THE
GAP
FACT

AND OUT-OF-WHACK
CREATION SCIENTISM

MICHAEL PEARL

First printing: August 2018

Print: ISBN: 978-1-61644-105-0
ePub: ISBN: 978-1-61644-106-7
ePDF: ISBN: 978-1-61644-107-4

All Scripture quotations are taken from the Authorized (King James) Holy Bible

1. Creation Science 2. The Gap Fact 3. The Gap Theory 4. Young Earth 5. Genesis
6. Evolution 7. Earth Age 8. Creation Scientist
I. Pearl, Michael II. The Gap Fact and Out-of-Whack Creation Scientism

The Gap Fact and Out-of-Whack Creation Scientism may be purchased at special quantity discounts for churches, donor programs, fund raising, book clubs, or educational purposes for churches, congregations, schools and universities. Rights and Licensing in other languages and international sales opportunities are available. For more information contact:

No Greater Joy Ministries
1000 Pearl Road
Pleasantville TN 37033
1-866-292-9936
ngj@nogreaterjoy.org

Printed in the United States of America

Publisher: No Greater Joy Ministries, Inc.
www.nogreaterjoy.org

CONTENTS

PREFACE

This author greatly appreciates the many works published by Creation Scientists as they bring the wonders and complexities of creation to life. They have done a great job of challenging the evolutionists and providing vacillating Christians with scientific proof of special creation. Our thanks go out to them. We appreciate the strong evidence they provide, demonstrating that much (if not all) of what secular geologists dub "great geological ages" is, in fact, a result of Noah's flood. That is a good debate for scientists to have, for it can be conducted on the grounds of empirical evidence. And there is an abundance of evidence for the effects of the Flood upon our geological history, just as there is evidence for a very old earth and universe.

HOWEVER, in their attempt to rid evolutionists of the time frame supposedly required for evolution to occur, they have tried to build an argument based on a 6,000- to 10,000-year-old universe—a concept impossible to validate by either science or the Bible. According to the Christian Science movement, just over 10,000 years ago there was no universe, no time, and no dimension. There was no light or darkness; nothing moved or changed. There was not even an empty space waiting to be filled. Nothing but God dwelling in a non-dimensional nothing for which there was no name and no description.

We don't fault them for believing this if they deem the evidence sufficient as long as they keep it in the science arena where hypotheses are made, theories are propounded, evidence is synthesized, and conclusions are subject to peer review. But we don't appreciate these Christian scientists meddling in the theological arena and faulting Bible believers for with-holding judgment as to the age of the earth. Neither do we appreciate the **intellectual roadblock** they have thrown up between our Christian witness and the average person who knows he has just viewed stars that are millions of light years away. Since God chose to create everything with the appearance of age, why blame geologists for discovering the evidence of age? Why blame other Creationists for not agreeing with disputable scientific opinion that the universe is only 6,000–10,000 years old when there is clear scriptural support for a universe older than the first six days of Genesis?

There is abundant documentation that the early Christians and Jews reading the Hebrew, Greek, Aramaic, and Latin texts believed that Genesis 1:1 recorded the creation of the earth and the universe prior to the beginning of the six days of creation. YET, the Young Earth Theory, a **modern invention** of scientists and pseudo-scientists, falsely asserts that what is now called the Gap Theory ". . . arose when Christian leaders tried to accommodate the millions of years claimed by scientific research which was done by unsaved geologists, for fossil layers."[1]

---

1   http://www.icr.org/article/108/314

When Young Earth Scientism asserts that the Gap Theory began in the 1800s, they ignore its historical underpinnings and refer only to the bastardized version. They are denigrating old-time Bible believers who believed in a gap long before anyone ever heard of evolution or geology. This is so easily proven that **I have a hard time believing they are unaware of the facts.** Did they think we couldn't research?

Ever since Moses wrote the book of Genesis, there have been astute biblical textualists who understood that heaven and earth were created in the beginning, before the six days of creation recorded in Genesis 1:3 and following. But it was seldom mentioned, just as no one mentioned the Young Earth Theory because the age of the earth was of little consequence to any subject other than the history of Lucifer and the angels. It wasn't until natural science advanced to the point of observing the age of the earth and universe that the time frame of Genesis became relevant. Then the doctrine of a gap was pulled from dusty old books to be endowed with new content by science-worshiping, geology-credentialed Christians who were intimidated by organic evolution.

The Creation Science movement has put out false propaganda, leading Christians who don't have a solid biblical or historical foundation to make a judgment without knowing all the facts. Young Earthers have seduced Christians with their "science," causing them to become judges of the Bible, rejecting long-standing, traditional doctrine and replacing it with faith in the suspect scientific interpretation of a few.

Disciples of these Young Earth Scientists, raised in this era of biblical ignorance, have succumbed to the flood (pun intended) of one-sided propaganda and have become militant in their assertions, denigrating and maligning traditional

Bible doctrine that has been the belief of Bible students for more than 2,000 years. They attempt to marginalize those who still hold to traditional belief. **Their single-issue fervency, holding out the Young Earth Theory as a litmus test for orthodoxy, has evolved into a new "ism" with cult-like intensity and zeal.** The time has come to expose it.

-Michael Pearl

It should be noted that we have quoted many websites to expose the fallacies of the non-gap belief. It is to be expected that these websites will change over the course of time but that they are accurate at the time of publishing this book, and that even though they may change they hold the view of many modern Christians.

Also, many quotes have been used in this book and **bold** font has been applied by this author to many of those quotes to emphasize different points.

CREATIONISM
has been hijacked by Young Earthism.

So there is a new ism
creating a schism
and the division
has induced a collision
and merited derision
that we did not envision
fifty years ago.

CHAPTER 1

THE WAY IT WAS,
BY ONE WHO WAS THERE

"Evolution: Science Falsely So-Called"

In 1966 when I was in Bible College, I stumbled out of Greek class overcome with consternation and into the school bookstore, where everything was in English, looking for emotional comfort. That is when the clerk, knowing I spent a lot of time preaching on the streets to college students, directed me to International Christian Crusade's little yellow booklet titled *Evolution: Science Falsely So-Called*. It confronted the subject of evolution on the grounds of science. I devoured the contents until I had practically memorized it. I then discovered *The Genesis Flood* by Henry Morris and John C. Whitcomb, published in 1961. It greatly expanded my appreciation for the science of Spoken Word Creation. I occasionally utilized the information to silence those who argued against the Bible from an evolutionary perspective.

It was fun to win an argument. But winning an argument on the basis of scientific knowledge does not equate with winning the person to Christ. At the time I could not imagine that Creation Science would become an enemy of the Word of God.

Through Faith We Understand

When I was a young man sixty years ago, we knew from the plain sense of Scripture that there was an indeterminate time gap between Genesis 1:1 and 1:3. Our belief had nothing to do with attempting to accommodate the supposed geological ages of evolution, nor were we attempting to provide time for the apparent age of the fossil record. Our belief was based solely on the text of the Holy Bible. Any professing Christian who believed in Day Age or Theistic Evolution was considered an infidel.

In the 1950s and early '60s, as far as I knew, all Bible believers readily understood that according to the Bible's chronology, about 6,000 years ago the Spirit of God moved upon the face of a lifeless planet that was without form and void, and there he commenced a creation week composed of six twenty-four-hour days. In those six days God spoke into existence this present ecosystem, including all plants, animals, and humans; and no process of evolution was employed. **"For he spake, and it was done; he commanded, and it stood fast"** (Psalm 33:9).

> **Exodus 20:11** For in six days the LORD made heaven and earth, the sea, and all that in them is, and rested the seventh day: wherefore the LORD blessed the sabbath day, and hallowed it.

Our confidence in Spoken Word Creation was not threatened by evolution, and we didn't feel the need to harmonize the biblical record with it. We believed God and that was enough. We just laughed at organic evolution and wondered how anyone could believe something so preposterous. We were able to win thousands of evolution-oriented college students to faith in Christ with the Bible alone. The message of Christ overcame their skepticism with very little attention to evolution.

When an unbeliever resisted the Bible by saying the earth was very old, we agreed and said something like: "Of course. God created it a long time ago and placed a race on it that we now know as angels. Some sinned and became devils and some didn't. God cursed the planet, destroying everything on it, and damned the fallen angels. About six thousand years ago God re-created this planet and replenished it with a new race that was not quite as smart or gifted as the first, and he gave us a free will so we could do as we pleased, but he offered the option to live in love and faith or to disobey and be damned like the angels that sinned. The fallen cherub entered paradise disguised as a recently created beast of the field. He spoke to Eve and informed her that God was preventing her from attaining special knowledge that would bring great fulfilment. Eve sinned, and then Adam chose to follow her in rebellion, taking his entire posterity with him. And that is why there is so much evil in the world, resulting in death and hell…But God who is rich in mercy…" And then with ten to twenty minutes of the gospel of Jesus, we had a new brother or sister in Christ. They stopped being evolutionists when they started believing Jesus was their savior, and **we never had to debate the age of the earth.**

We didn't care what they believed about geology; the issue was the integrity of the gospel narrative, for it had power to win hearts first and then minds. I saw it happen hundreds—maybe thousands—of times. In recent years working in the prisons, I have observed the same results. When you give people Jesus, they forget the crutch of evolution without ever looking back. Evolution never made sense to them either, not even to their professors. They just assumed it because it was the only alternative to a legislating creator.

Seashells and Sand

In the days before the arrival of Scientific Creationism and the Young Earth Theory with its "one size fits all" attempt to answer geology and evolution, we simple believers knew that everything God created, regardless of how long ago, was created with the **appearance of age.** One second after creation, all the trees had annual growth rings varying according to their designed age. All vegetation was in various stages of development, appearing to be aged, some of it already matured and falling to the ground to decompose, providing nutrients for budding seedlings. The beach was covered with sand, as occurs over a period of time through the grinding action of surf. And old shells were strewn along the beach with hermit crabs peeking out here and there. The sea had the proper amount of salt as if erosion had been occurring for millions of years. Coral reefs were in place, teeming with new life representing every stage of development. The moon was cratered, and streams showed erosion in the rounded, water-washed rocks and sand—and all this just one second after creation.

The Chicken or the Egg?

Remember the philosophical question, "Which came first, the chicken or the egg?" A Spoken Word Creationist answers, "Both." A hen shedding old feathers was created sitting on an egg that was halfway through its incubation cycle, while a young and an old rooster fought over six hens in various stages of maturity, and another hen was leading her twelve little chicks down to the water where there were tadpoles that appeared to be two weeks old swimming around water reeds that had just blossomed and were being pollinated by bees whose hive was already half full of honey. The little chicks pecked at the fallen seeds and partly decomposed fruit until their attention turned to the tempting but elusive tadpoles. It was all in a day's work—or I should say, six days. It could not be otherwise in this complex, interdependent ecosystem.

God Makes New Antiques

We know that the earth and universe were created with the appearance of age. To believe otherwise is to believe in some form of progressive creation or evolution, regardless of how you arrange the pieces. There is no other alternative for anyone who believes in Spoken Word Creation. This interdependent system must be activated fully intact for the individual parts to survive. It is aptly called "irreducible complexity." The greater miracle would be Theistic Evolution over a great period of time, for in this irreducibly complex system God would have to keep the clock ticking while he waited millions of years to create the parts necessary for it to tick. Why employ an absurdly complicated and counter-productive mechanism to achieve creation? For life-forms to evolve into more complex organisms over an extended period of time, it would entail a new work of creation (something from nothing) on a daily basis. Doing it that way, God would use up additional creation energy. Is creation so hard for God that he had to work his way into it one little piece at a time? Either God is the Instant Spoken Word Creator, or he is a Theistic Evolutionist who created one piece at a time, supernaturally sustaining the individual parts that depend upon the yet-uncreated parts to survive.

Nature is a balance of competing forces, from the atom with its positive and negative charges to the ecosystem filled with rival fungi, enzymes, plants, insects, and animals, all dependent upon the mature function of the whole. An enzyme without a balancing enzyme would destroy a living organism. A flower without insects to pollinate it would not survive. Soil without composted matter to provide nutrients would not sustain the plants that depended upon it. God is either an organic farmer, creating a system that is self-reliant and self-sustaining or he is a Monsanto-chemical kind of Theistic Evolutionary creator who creates a little at a time and applies artificial fertilizer to feed the plants until sufficient composted material is generated to sustain them naturally. And he would have to manually pollinate the plants until he decided to create myriads of insects that depend upon the pollen for survival. Instant Spoken Word Creation with built-in age is the only possibility regardless of when the earth was created, be it six thousand or six billion years ago. Otherwise God would be exhausted and bored for years trying to keep a partial system functioning. Would an internal combustion motor run with only half of the parts assembled?

So it is **nothing new to believe in God creating with the appearance of age.** He made new antiques. If they look old, all credit goes to the craftsmanship of the Creator. If you don't think they are old, you will have a hard time proving it. He is just that good at making new things look old.

When God created the stars of heaven, he didn't wait one hundred million years for the light to reach his position. When he said, "Let there be light," there was instant light all the way from the source to all corners of the universe. Astronomers have viewed stars nine billion light years away.

That means that the light source they are viewing was there at that spot nine billion years ago. It may be long gone by now. To see that star as it is today one would have to wait another nine billion years. When you view the universe, you are looking at very old, archived images. When God spoke the universe into existence, **he spoke its past into existence as well**, creating the light in transit to all points in the universe. And since all things were created with the appearance of age, there is no way to determine the age of the universe or this ecosystem by the scientific process, for you must make certain assumptions about the uniformity and constancy of certain "laws" of nature for the scientific process to be reliable. The only thing a scientist can do is determine how old God made it **appear** to be. One minute after Adam was created, his teeth showed the normal wear from chewing, his toenails needed clipping, and—of practical necessity—his feet came equipped with calluses.

The Devil in the Details

Back in the days when Christians never doubted that every word of their Bible was inspired by God, a simple reading informed us that Lucifer and all the angels were present when the earth was created, for they "sang together, and… shouted for joy" (Job 38:6–7) as they observed the foundations of the earth being laid.

Kids in Sunday school knew that Lucifer's sin predated Eve's in that he was in the garden tempting Eve shortly after creation. Due to his disembodied state, it was necessary for him to commandeer the body of a "beast of the field" in order to manifest a physical presence and speak to Eve. Satan had lost his original physical body in death following his sin (Psalm 82:6–7; Ezekiel 14:12–17; Isaiah 28:17).

So we cannot do other than conclude that Lucifer was created before the earth, sinned before the six days, met with the wages of sin—which is death—before Adam, and was found in the garden as a sinner tempting Eve shortly after re-creation. Kids' stuff. We will examine the issue of death before Adam later.

Having Done All, to Stand

When I was a teenager, Bible-believing Christians paid little attention to the battle raging in academia and went on as usual, shouting and praying-through in our revival meetings, and singing "Oh, thou great Creator." We could accept a young earth, an old earth, or a half-old earth. It didn't matter to us one way or the other. We were more concerned about young converts and old fogies who got tired after two hours of singing, praying, and preaching.

We believers in Spoken Word Creation have stood fast from the beginning on through the nineteenth and twentieth centuries, and into the twenty-first, believing in the inspiration and preservation of the Word of God, which tells us of a six-day creation that occurred on a previously existing planet that came to be without form and void. We never paid any attention to "science falsely so called" in the past and will not do so now. Here we stand; we cannot do otherwise.

Personal

I have shared my personal perspective as one who was part of mainstream conservative Christianity in the 1950s and '60s. I am well aware that while I believed all was well, outside of my circle, in neo-evangelical institutions and apostate churches across America and around the world, the conservative viewpoint was giving way to an exaltation of science and psychology and a dismissal of the Bible as the infallible words of God. But the faithful church of Christ has always had a constant drip of apostasy from its ranks. There were those who stopped believing in Spoken Word Creation but continued as college professors and pastors, because their livelihood was tied up in religion.

You may think I came from a small, naïve sect of fundamentalist Christianity, not representative of the whole. That is partly true. But I can assure you my perspective in 1965 was typical of all conservative Christianity where a normal, grammatical approach to interpretation was employed.

For in 1954, noted theologian and writer Bernard Ramm, **who did not believe** in Spoken Word Creation nor the traditional view of the Gap, wrote in *The Christian View of Science and Scripture*:

> "The gap theory has become **the standard interpretation throughout hyper-orthodoxy,** appearing in an endless stream of books, booklets, Bible studies, and periodical articles. In fact, it has become so sacrosanct with some that **to question it is equivalent to tampering with Sacred Scripture** or to manifest modernistic leanings." (p. 135)

When Ramm referred to hyper-orthodoxy, he meant those who say "God said it and that settles it." To avoid this label, one must harmonize his biblical interpretation with science— which equates to becoming a Theistic Evolutionist. In other words, from Ramm's perspective, the Gap Theory was the standard interpretation of Bible believers in 1954, making us HYPER-orthodox. We relied solely on the Bible and did not believe in any form of evolution. Ramm was not aware of the

Young Earth crowd, for it was a heresy waiting to be birthed from an illicit affair between Creationists and science.

The truth is that the Gap had always been the standard interpretation all the way back to the ancient, Hebrew-reading Jews.

Little did we know in 1965 that it would be "orthodox" Christians themselves who would attack the words of God as they were historically understood and eventually discredit the Bible in the eyes of secularists with their Young Earth Theory!

CHAPTER 2

ANCIENT GAP
CREATIONISTS

New Idea?

Young Earth Theorism, a recent development in the scientific theology department, of all things asserts that the doctrine of Gap Creationism is a new idea developed in the nineteenth century to accommodate evolution and make room for the geological ages. Christiananswers.net expresses the Young Earth Theory (YET) sentiment in "What is the 'Gap Theory'?"

> "Western Bible commentaries written before the 18th century, and before the belief in a long age for the Earth became popular, **knew nothing of any gap** between Genesis 1:1 and Genesis 1:2."[1]

---

1   https://christiananswers.net/q-aig/aig-c003.html

The author says, they **"knew nothing of any gap."** We will prove otherwise.

They also assert that Gap Creationism is **"A marginal view few have ever heard of."** If that is a measure of anything, be it known that few to none had ever heard of the Young Earth Theory before 1961. Tom Mclver in "Formless and Void: Gap Theory Creationism" (published in *Creation Evolution Journal*, 1988, Vol. 8), says that *The Genesis Flood* by John Whitcomb and Henry Morris, first published in 1961, is **"largely responsible for the revival of Flood geology and young-earth creationism."**

Here we are just sixty-four years after Ramm's statement, and a group of scientists (ICR—Institute for Creation Research) are telling us that we are **unorthodox** for believing what all the orthodox believed until modern times. How things do change where "science falsely so called" covets the prophet's mantle and tries to tell Bible readers what to believe, and then tries to rewrite our history of belief.

In 1988 Tom Mclver, NOT a Gap advocate, says, **"Odd it may be, but the gap theory was—and still is—widely believed"** (*"Formless and Void,"* p. 4).

It is wishful thinking to suggest that the Gap Doctrine is a marginal view. It is unknown and unappreciated only by those who know very little of the Bible in regard to any subject, and very little of history, which is a large segment of modern Christianity.

A New Idea in 1491 BC

The Gap fact was first revealed in a publication in 1491 BC when God dictated Genesis 1 to Moses on Mt. Sinai. We will discuss the Scripture later. But since we are writing about ancient views of the Gap, it is essential to include the very first mention—Genesis 1:1–2. I will now provide irrefutable proof that Gap Creationism is the oldest of views.

First and Second Centuries

Though it was seldom a point of discussion, the concept of a gap was common among ancient Hebrew rabbis. Akiba ben Joseph, who was executed by the Romans in 135 AD, left a clear witness in what would become known as the Mishna. One of Akiba's disciples, Simeon ben Jochai, wrote *The Book of Light*, or *Zohar*. His commentary on Genesis 2:4–6 expresses the common view held during the lifetime of the apostles and into the second century.

> "These are the generations of heaven and earth…
> Now wherever there is written the word 'these'
> (אלה) the previous words are put aside. And these
> are the generations of the destruction which is
> signified in verse 2 of chapter 1. The earth was Tohu
> and Bohu. These indeed are the worlds of which
> it is said that the blessed God created them and
> destroyed them, and, on that account, the earth was
> desolate and empty."

This ancient writer who was contemporaneous with the early church had no agenda other than interpreting the Hebrew Scriptures, a living language in his day. The text itself forces the conclusion that the heaven (not heavens) and earth were created at some point prior to Genesis 1:3 and became "empty and desolate" (without form and void) through an act of judgment. Yet today, men who are able to shop for an opinion among a number of Hebrew lexicons—though the authors couldn't order a bowl of lentils in West Jerusalem— have the audacity to spout Hebrew meanings that contradict the ancient Hebrew scholars of the first century. Pick your favorite lexicon. I will stick with the text of the inspired words of God and appreciate the ancient writers who did the same.

Jewish Midrash

Arthur C. Custance (MA in Hebrew and Greek and PhD in biblical archeology and anthropology) was a Canadian anthropologist, scientist, and author specializing in science and Christianity. In 1970 he privately published *Without Form and Void.*

> "We are in no position at present to determine precisely how the Jewish commentators made the discovery, but their early literature (the Midrash for example) reveals that they had some intimation of an early pre-Adamic catastrophe affecting the whole earth. Similarly, clear evidence appears in the oldest extant Version of the Hebrew Scriptures (the Targum of Onkelos) and some intimation may be seen in the "punctuation marks" of the Masoretic text of Genesis, Chapter One." (p. 2–3)

The Jewish Midrash, originating after the Babylonian captivity, over 500 years **before** Christ, contains early interpretations and commentaries on the Hebrew Bible. It was the basis of rabbinical teaching at the time of Christ. A copy of it was found in the Dead Sea Scrolls, predating the New Testament. There are other preserved copies dating from the second century AD, just decades after the apostles. The Midrash is a highly respected exegesis of the Hebrew Bible from various perspectives by many writers and traditions, providing us with a history of their understanding of the text. How could modern writers dare suggest that Gap Creationism is a new idea designed to accommodate modern evolutionary thinking when we have clear records of its antiquity?

Custance Has More to Say

"A few of the early Church Fathers accepted this interpretation and based some of their doctrines upon it."

"The truth is, as we shall see, that the idea of a once ordered world having been brought to ruin as a consequence of divine judgment just prior to the creation of Adam, was apparently quite widespread. It was not debated: it was merely held by some and not by others."

"In short, it is not a recent interpretation of the text of Gen. 1.1 and 1.2, but an ancient one long antedating modern geological views." (*Without Form and Void*, p. 3)

Those closest to the Hebrew Bible, reflecting the historical understanding of the text from at least five centuries before Christ, understood the text to be suggesting the earth existed in a chaotic state prior to the six days of creation.

Isn't it time to stop fooling the people, making them think the Creation Gap Doctrine is of recent origin?

Aramaic Old Testament

Custance highlights "substantiating evidence" in the "Targum of Onkelos, the earliest of the Aramaic Versions of the Old Testament written by Hebrew Scholars." It dates to around the end of the first century or earlier, possibly contemporaneous with the Apostle John. Custance says:

"We have here, therefore, a rendering '**and the earth was laid waste,**' an interpretation of the original Hebrew of Gen. 1:2 which leaves little room for doubt that Onkelos understood this to mean that **something had occurred between verse**

1 and verse 2 to reduce the earth to this desolated condition." (*Without Form and Void*, p. 5–6)

Think about it. A few decades after the apostles, Hebrew commentators, perpetuating their oral and written traditions, translate the text to say **"the earth was laid waste."** How could modern Young Earth enthusiasts ignore this ancient record, claiming it is a new doctrine invented to accommodate evolution?

Origen Adamantius (186–254 AD)

Origen, in spite of his infidelity to the sacredness of Scripture, was quite familiar with the original languages as well as a number of related languages. He was head of the Royal Library of Alexandria, Egypt, founded in the third century before Christ. At its height it contained an estimated 400,000 volumes from all over the known world in many languages. In his work *De Principiis*, commenting on Genesis 1:1, Origen says:

> "It is certain that the present firmament is not spoken of in this verse, nor the present dry land, but rather that heaven and earth from which this present heaven and earth that we now see afterwards borrowed their names." (*Without Form and Void*, p. 9)

With no agenda and a complete knowledge of the Hebrew Bible and Hebrew commentaries, Origen interprets the original text to be teaching a gap just as it had always been believed by Bible students who had no agenda other than understanding the text.

Augustine, Fourth & Fifth Centuries AD

Everyone is familiar with fourth- and fifth-century Augustine. He wrote in his *Confessions* (397–400 AD) that which was commonly believed in his day. Please note, this is **more than fourteen centuries before Darwin,** about three hundred years after the death of the last apostle.

"Chapter VIII—Heaven and Earth were made 'In the beginning;' afterwards the world, during six days, from shapeless matter.

For very wonderful is this corporeal heaven; of which firmament between water and water, the second day, after the creation of light, Thou saidst, Let it be made, and it was made. Which firmament Thou callest heaven; the heaven, that is, to this earth and sea, which Thou madest the third day, by giving a visible figure to the formless matter, **which Thou madest before all days.** For **already hadst Thou made both an heaven, before all days**; but that was the heaven of this heaven; because In the beginning Thou hadst made heaven and earth. But this same earth which Thou madest was formless matter, because it was invisible and without form, and darkness was upon the deep…" (*The Confessions of Saint Augustine,* Chapter VIII)

He said that the **"heaven of this heaven"** was **"made before all days** *[the six days]*." Augustine was not confronted with any form of geology nor any scientific challenge that would have motivated him to promote an old earth as some form of compromise. He was simply exegeting the Scripture in the original language as he understood it, consistent with past commentators.

Young Earth Scientism ignores the many examples of Hebrews and Christians who believed in the Gap thousands of years before Darwin or his kind. Either critics of the Gap have failed to actually investigate OR they are being dishonest with the evidence. Not very scientific either way.

In due course you will read all the Scripture that proves the reality of an earth existing before the six days of creation, and we will answer all the major arguments of the argumentative.

King Edgar of England (943–975)

Erich Sauer was author of a number of well-received books, especially *The Dawn of World Redemption*—a book well worth reading. According to Sauer, King Edgar of England expressed his belief in an earth older than the six days of re-creation.

Hugo St. Victor (1097–1141)

Custance provides us with a quote from Hugo St. Victor of the twelfth century:

> "Perhaps enough has already been debated about these matters thus far, if we add only this, **how long did the world remain in this disorder before the regular re-ordering** (disposition) of it was taken in hand? For the fact that the first substance of all things arose at the very beginning of time—or rather, with time itself—is settled by the statement that, 'In the beginning God created the heavens and the earth'. But how long it continued in this state of confusion, Scripture does not clearly show." (*Without Form and Void,* p. 12; *De Sacramentis Christianae Fidei,* Book 1, part 1, chapter 6)

Wow! He not only believed in a gap, he revealed that it was a matter of significant debate. And he referred to the six days of creation as a "**re-ordering**" of the former creation.

Thomas Aquinas (1225–1274)

Thomas Aquinas is a well-known and highly respected name even in secular circles. He is known for his ideas on philosophy from a Christian perspective, ethics, and his views on natural law and political theory. Custance quotes Aquinas on the Creation Gap:

> "...but it seems better to maintain (the view) that the **creation was prior to any of the days** (literally, before any day)." (*Without Form and Void*, p. 12)

Dionysius Petavius (1583–1652)

A French Roman Catholic Jesuit theologian who was first professor of philosophy at Bourges and later professor of theology at Paris, wrote:

> "The question of how great an interval there was, it is not possible except by inspiration to attain knowledge of." (*Without Form and Void*, p. 13–14)

And So Forth

Many highly respected scholars of the 1700s advocated for Gap Creationism: Arnold Fruchtenbaum, Robert Lightner, J. C. Rosenmüller (1776), Johann August Dathe (about 1731–1791), and others wrote of a gap.

There were many additional early church and medieval commentators who wrote of a gap, but the ones listed are more than enough to prove the antiquity of Gap Creationism. Listing more would just be rubbing it in.

Adam Clarke (1763–1832)

Clarke, a British Methodist theologian and Bible scholar, in his *Adam Clarke Commentary*, Genesis 1:2, expresses the common interpretation of Genesis 1:1–3 at that time.

Clarke, a Hebrew scholar, reflects the view held by the ancient Hebrews as well as Bible-believing Christians down through the ages, that the creation of the heaven and earth occurred sometime before the six days' creation.

> "The earth was without form and void - The original term תהו tohu and בהו bohu, which we translate without form and void, are of uncertain etymology; but in this place, and wherever else they are used, they convey the idea of confusion and disorder.
>
> God seems at first to have created the elementary principles of all things; and this formed the grand mass of matter, which in this state must be without arrangement, or any distinction of parts: a vast collection of indescribably confused materials, of nameless entities strangely mixed...
>
> The most ancient of the Greeks have spoken nearly in the same way of this crude, indigested state of the primitive chaotic mass.
>
> When this congeries of elementary principles was brought together, God was pleased to spend six days in assimilating, assorting, and arranging the materials, out of which he built up, not only the earth, but the whole of the solar system."

I am not suggesting that his views carry through to the concept of a former paradise falling into ruin to be rebuilt, only that he understood the text to separate the original creation of heaven and earth from the six days of re-creation.

John Nelson Darby (1800–1882)

Darby was an Anglo-Irish Bible teacher, one of the influential figures among the original Plymouth Brethren and the founder of the Exclusive Brethren. He produced translations of the Bible in German (Elberfelder Bibel), the French "Pau" Bible, a Dutch New Testament, and an English translation (finished posthumously) based on the Hebrew and Greek texts called *The Holy Scriptures: A New Translation from the Original Languages.* It has furthermore been translated into other languages in whole or part.[1] This learned scholar was an avid Gap Creationist.

C. H. Spurgeon (1855)

C. H. Spurgeon's sermon *The Power of the Holy Ghost,* published in 1855 **four years before** Darwin's *Origin of the Species,* demonstrates a clear understanding of an older earth.

> "We know not how remote the creation of this earth may be; **certainly millions of years before the time of Adam.** Our planet has passed through various stages of existence, and different kinds of creatures have lived on its surface, all of which have been fashioned by God. But before that era came, wherein man should be its principal tenant and monarch, the **Creator gave up the world to confusion.** He allowed the inward fires to burn up from beneath and melt all the solid matter so that all kinds of substances were commingled in one vast massive disorder."

Answers in Genesis published this sermon on its website but **deleted the above remarks** that revealed Spurgeon's support for the Gap. After several people noticed, it became a point of public embarrassment and they restored the edited section.

---

1   https://en.wikipedia.org/wiki/John_Nelson_Darby

"Can any man tell me when the beginning was?
Years ago we thought the beginning of this world
was when Adam came upon it; but we have
discovered that thousands of years before that
God was preparing chaotic matter to make it a fit
abode for man, **putting races of creatures upon
it**, who might die and leave behind the marks
of his handiwork and marvelous skill, before he
tried his hand on man."

Several articles and web-based defenses of Young Earthism
list the many scholars who did **not** believe in a gap. It is **odd
that Spurgeon is often included as a no-Gapist** when he
is on record repeatedly expressing confidence in it. In fact,
Spurgeon was a little bit of a neo-evangelical in the making.

William Kelly (1821–1906)

Kelly, like John Nelson Darby, was a very competent Hebrew
and Greek scholar who produced translations (not para-
phrases) of books of the Bible from the original languages,
along with numerous in-depth commentaries on Scripture.
Gap Creationism is well supported in his writings.

Merrill F. Unger (1909–1980)

Unger was a Bible commentator, highly acclaimed scholar,
archaeologist, and theologian who earned his BA and PhD
degrees at Johns Hopkins. He notes the original perfect
condition had been ruined by the sin of the earth's former
angelic inhabitants.

"The majestic opening verse of Genesis: 'In the beginning God created the heavens and earth,' apparently
does not refer to the original sinless and perfect earth
brought into existence in dim antiquity. That origi-

nal sphere, says Isaiah, was created 'not a waste' but 'formed to be inhabited' (Isaiah 45:18). The laying of its cornerstone was celebrated by the sinless song of 'the morning stars' and the joyous shouts of 'all the sons of God' (angels), perhaps millions of years ago." ("Rethinking the Genesis Account of Creation," *Bibliotheca Sacra,* 1958)

J. Vernon McGee (1904–1988)

McGee earned his ThM and ThD from Dallas Theological Seminary and came to be perhaps the most popular radio Bible teacher of all times with a program called *Thru the Bible.* It was translated and re-broadcast in over a hundred languages. His radio ministry began in 1941 and continues to this day.

"The Bible seems to teach in Isaiah 45:18 that God didn't create the earth in this state originally, and that something happened later to cause the chaotic state." (*Thru the Bible,* Vol. 1, Gen.–Deut., p. 13)

Dr. H. A. Ironside (1876–1951)

"Could the whole universe, including the earth, have looked like the moon and other planets in our solar system when God brought judgment upon the original earth?" (*Dr. Ironside's Bible,* p. 25)

To dismiss all these influential teachers and scholars as attempting to accommodate the geological ages of evolution is ludicrous to say the least.

Arthur Pink (1886–1952)

Pink had much to say in support of the Gap (*Gleanings in Genesis,* p. 10).

Donald Grey Barnhouse (1895–1960)
Barnhouse was twice elected president of the Southern Baptist Convention from 1968 to 1970. See his book *Genesis* (p. 10) where he speaks of the Gap. In addition, a major portion of his book *The Invisible War* is about the Gap.

Arno C. Gaebelein (1861–1945)
See his *The Annotated Bible*, p. 16–17.

E. Schuyler English (1899–1981)
See his edition of *Pilgrim Study Bible,* p. 1 footnotes.

Lewis Sperry Chafer (1871–1952)
Chafer was founder and president of Dallas Theological Seminary and often made reference to the Gap between Genesis 1:1 and 1:3.

W. A. Criswell (1909–2002)
Criswell was pastor of the First Baptist Church in Dallas, Texas, with 26,000 in weekly attendance. He was twice elected president of the Southern Baptist Convention. His dispensationalism and adherence to Gap Creationism were well known. See his *Great Doctrines of the Bible*, Vol. 7, Prayer/Angelology, p. 89.

Many Additional Renowned Scholars
G. H. Pember, C. S. Lewis, M. R. DeHaan, Francis Schaeffer, and others too numerous to mention all believed in the doctrine of the Gap. In fact, in 1960 you would be hard pressed to find any well-known preacher who did not believe in the Gap.

Confirmation from the Other Side
J. E. Smith does not believe in the Gap; nonetheless, in his

Old Testament Survey Series he admits that Gap Creationism is not a new concept hatched by Christians seeking to harmonize Scripture with evolution. He says it was a prominent view long before the discovery of prehistoric fossils.

> "Opponents of the Gap Theory often contend that it has been superimposed upon Genesis as a means of harmonizing the existence of prehistoric fossils alleged to be millions of years old on the one hand, and a Biblical chronology which measures the creation of Adam in thousands and not millions of years. **Advocates of the Gap Theory, however, long antedate the discovery of prehistoric fossils.**" (*The Pentateuch*)

D. G. Lindsay, does not believe in a gap, nevertheless is honest in his analysis of the evidence.

> "Can Genesis 1:2 be translated "Now the earth *became* waste and void"? Many authorities insist that the verb *hayah* cannot be rendered *became* here. The truth of the matter is that this verb more often than not expresses an action and not a state of being. **The Gap Theory cannot be opposed on linguistic grounds.**" (*The Dinosaur Dilemma: Fact or Fantasy*).

The purpose of this chapter was to answer the charge that Gap Creationism is an obscure doctrine of late origin. We have proven our critics false to the highest level of certitude.

CHAPTER 3

HOW DID THE GAP CONTROVERSY ARISE?

Understanding the Conflict

Galileo, often called the father of modern science, started modern scientific development in 1615 AD when he promoted Copernicus' heliocentric (sun at the center of our solar system) rather than geocentric (earth at the center) celestial system. Both the Roman Catholic Church and the newly formed Protestants were rabidly anti-science. **Roman Catholic Inquisitors** found him "vehemently suspect of heresy," and when he refused to print a publication proving the error of his position, he was imprisoned and later transferred to house arrest where his scientific research and pronouncements could be censored as needed for the rest of his life.

The anti-science sentiment didn't go away with the advent of Protestantism. Martin Luther's coworker Philipp

Melanchthon wrote, "certain people believe it is a marvelous achievement to extol so crazy a thing *[heliocentrism]*, like that Polish astronomer *[Copernicus]* who makes the earth move and the sun stand still. Really, wise governments ought to repress impudence of mind." This leading churchman was ready to support government suppression of science, because he entertained the Reformed Church notion that the earth was the center of the universe. He apparently thought he had it on divine authority.

Events like this created a rift between science and religion, and understandably so. Science had gone through the Dark Ages and all the way into the sixteenth and seventeenth centuries weighed down by the reluctance of religious institutions to accept scientific research and discovery, and even hostility toward it.

You must understand that people of faith were not the enemies of science. They **WERE** the scientists. It was structured Christianity—Roman Catholicism and Reformed Catholicism, otherwise known as Calvinism—that stood against free thinking in its own ranks. Most of the early advances in natural sciences were by Christian scholars who had to dance around Rome and religious dogma to advance their ideas: men like John Philoponus 490–570 AD, Paul of Aegina 625–690, the Venerable Bede 672–735, Roger Bacon 1214–94, Thomas Aquinas 1227–74, and the list goes on. Just research medieval scientific discoveries and you will see that it would be accurate to call early scientific discoveries "Christian discoveries."

With the many scientific advancements in the 1600s and 1700s, natural law took the place of what structured religion had represented as an unpredictable deity instigating every storm, earthquake, and celestial event. Science was no longer subject to censorship by church dogma. The world suddenly made sense like a piece of machinery—all the parts working together supporting one another, dependable, predictable. Science seemed to provide an explanation for everything, something religion had failed to do. The power of ecclesiastical superstition was swept aside by the wonders of natural law.

The West breathed fresh air as it was freed from the unreasonableness of religious dictates, and every decade brought new discoveries. It was an exciting time. There was an exuberance and sense of wonder at the ordered universe. Logic, law, chemistry, mathematics, philosophy, astronomy, and geology took the place of popes and priests with their unsupported dogmas. Government disentangled itself from the church, shaking off the darkness it had foisted on academics.

Keep in mind that the true local church, not part of Catholicism or Protestantism, continued on in faith, not meddling in politics or science, living righteously, not seeking to control anyone, nor to dictate policy. These believers were a succession of the earliest church, faithful and often persecuted unto death by both the Catholic Church and the Reformation Church (Lutherans and Calvinists). Most commonly they were called Anabaptists, but there were many names attached to them by their critics. Their views were not affected by geology or evolution. They continued as they had from the days of the apostles, "avoiding profane and vain babblings, and oppositions of science falsely so called" (1 Timothy 6:20).

Meanwhile, in the minds of many, beginning in the early 1700s, **science began to take the place of religion**. In academia and "cultured" society there was a wave of atheism and a libertine abandonment. Yet even with the advance of humanism and secularism, the idea that everything was the product of the Creator still held sway, for at the time there was no alternative.

Then in 1859 Darwin finally popularized a theory that could dethrone deity with his naturalistic explanation for creation itself. There was no Creator, just unintentional random chance. But it was a well-received idea because it allowed folk to live without judgment, without guilt, without fear of a day of reckoning. "Free at last, free at last; thank Random Selection Almighty, we're free at last."

Just for Perspective

This wave of independence from religion had another effect. As the discoveries in geology challenged the scientific accuracy of the Bible, biblical textual critics challenged the accuracy of the historical Greek text that had been the basis of the many language translations since the early church. With Westcott and Hort's newly created Greek Text (1881) proffered as a "better, more accurate Greek text," some gullible Christian leaders came to doubt the integrity of their Bibles. This unbelief exalted the "**science** of textual criticism" above faith in the words of God as found in the traditional Greek text and its translations. The "scientific" approach to Scripture continues unabated today with the publication of hundreds of English versions of the Bible, all differing from all others by at least 10%. The Bible text became fluid as it flowed between the fingers of unbelievers who hated the authority it had wielded for 1800 years. Ask any modernist preacher today to place in your hand a book wherein every word is the word of God, without error, and watch his reaction. He doesn't believe any such book exists upon the earth. There are exceptions, but when you find them, you will discover that they are probably Gap Creationists.

With religion suspect and the Bible in question, the faith of many shifted to the sciences. Thus began a **shift away from faith in the Bible to faith in the power of science**. Here we are less than two hundred years later, and those who put away God for science have now lost their faith in science. Many stare into space waiting to be saved by an alien race. Most just text and tweet and dawdle. The world has escaped reason and lives from day to day seeking the greatest pleasure before passing into the blackness of nothingness.

A segment of the church is doing what it has always done in times of public disregard when it has lost the power of the gospel: it has turned to apologetics, seeking to win the minds of thinkers. But there are no more thinkers—just unbelievers.

SO… How Did the Gap Controversy Arise?

How did this controversy arise between Young Earth Theorists and historical Gap Creationists? To fully understand it we must go back to a much earlier time.

You have read many historical examples of belief in a gap, dating back to the early church and beyond. But in the 1600s, the average Christian was not aware of these ancient writers. Few professional ministers would have been informed. Printing was new, and books were expensive. Remember, the Authorized Version was published in 1611. There were many, much more important issues at the forefront—things like justification by faith and the structure and authority of the local church. Little was known of the rapture or the millennium or dispensations.

Recently recovering from the Dark Ages of Roman imposed ignorance, the structured church (Protestantism) was rediscovering all its fundamental doctrines. In the 1600s, if a scholar had been reading an ancient writer and came across a comment on the Gap he probably would not have taken notice, for there was no concern as to the timing of creation. What was there to say? The Creation week (24-hour days) started with the angels already existing from some time in the past; the earth existed in darkness, and on the first day God turned on his work light so the angels could see until the fourth day when he created the sun.

Arthur C. Custance confirmed the early popularity of the Gap Creation view, saying that by virtue of the volume of witnesses **"it was apparently quite widespread"** *(Without Form and Void*, p. 3). Though it was widespread, it was not a subject of much interest other than a sidebar to commentaries on Genesis or an examination of the history of angels.

Ussher's Chronology Sets the Stage

The West emerged out of the religious Dark Ages hungry for knowledge. With the wide distribution of the Authorized Version (1611), literacy became common in England (near 90% for men) and there was a great demand for commentaries and Bible aids.

In the mid-1600s, James Ussher, the Archbishop of Armagh (Church of Ireland), compiled and published a chronology of the Bible based on the dates stated within the biblical text itself. He determined that Creation occurred 4004 BC. He was not attempting to make a scientific statement about the age of the earth; his goal was to provide a Bible-study tool that enabled students to organize the material in a **historical chronology.**

At the time, in the early to mid-1600s, there was no debate concerning Gap Creationism. Ussher's work was not an attempt to prove a young earth. Some just assumed the earth and universe to be young; others assumed it was older than the six days of Genesis. But because of the popularity of Ussher's chronology and a lack of discussion either way, over time most laymen and churchmen defaulted to the idea of a young earth. They didn't argue it or try to prove it. They couldn't tell you why they believed it, other than that Ussher said so. It was not relevant to any other belief and was not thought worthy of further development.

Ussher's chronology soon became the standard for all Christendom and has since been confirmed by many to accurately depict Bible dating. Ussher's chronology remains justifiably popular today.

Ussher's work was so influential that in 1700 if you had asked the average churchman how old the earth was, he would most likely have answered "fifty-seven hundred years." In the 1800s, with Bible students and secularists alike aware of the widely assumed belief of a 5800-year-old Creation, the stage was set for a confrontation between the soon-emerging field of geology and the church.

Geology, Supposology, and Theology

From about 1700 to 1780 AD, field geology, conducted mainly by Christian professionals, observed and documented the record of earth's geography as structured by natural processes and concluded that the changes occurred over a great period of time. By the early 1800s, it was generally accepted that this planet had a history that reached far beyond Ussher's 5800 years.

By the late 1800s, physicists had developed more sophisticated tools to observe and gauge the apparent age of the earth and the heavenly bodies. Estimates ranged from the upper millions to billions of years old. Remember, the early findings of geology were before Darwin and were not influenced by evolutionary thinking. But since it was well known that the "church" generally proclaimed the earth to be less than 6,000 years old, a conflict between religion and science was inevitable.

Before advances in geology, in the 1700s there was no provocation to view the Gap in creation as a great period of time. Students knew that there had to be enough time to account for the creation and history of angels and cherubim, and the subsequent fall of Satan and his angels, and for the earth to become without form and void where it awaited the six-day re-creation of Genesis 1:3, but few attempted to insert great ages, for the Bible does not reveal the time between Genesis 1:1 and 1:3. And there was no reason to think it was millions of years old. **No one dogmatically espoused belief in a young earth, nor in an old earth**. It was of no concern to anyone until the early to mid-1800s when the theologian, assuming a young earth, found his back up against the wall by the conclusions of geology.

The Evolution of Confusion—
The Day Age Theory

In the early to mid-1800s, with the church thinking the earth was 5800 years old and science thinking it was millions of years old, most churchmen were overwhelmed with the loss of prestige as science claimed the high ground of reasonableness. Christian academics, many of whom were credentialed in the various sciences, tried to beat the Bible critics at their own game by employing the very tools of science to validate the Bible.

The question was, how could the earth be billions of years old and the book of Genesis be taken literally? Seeking harmony between Genesis and the Geological Age Theory, compromising Christian academics seized upon the old, well-established but—in some circles—little-known view of a gap to insert millions of years into each day. It was a feeble attempt to allow time for evolution to take place under the guiding hand of the Not-So-Almighty. These apostate Christian academics crumbled under peer pressure and resorted to what would be called the Day Age Theory, supposing that God is the creator but that the days of creation were each perhaps millions of years long so as to allow for the geological developments to occur.

Thus was born Theistic Evolution—an untenable crossbreed. To adapt a phrase I heard somewhere: Crossing evolution and creation is like crossing a crocodile with an abalone; you get a crocabaloney.

But with the crock-of-baloney maneuver, Christian geologists saved their jobs, their academic reputations, and their religion. They could continue to be "Christians" and remain scientifically up to date, thus avoiding ridicule from their peers—for a while. There is nothing professionals fear so much as ridicule from their peers. But the compromisers got lost somewhere in Never Never Land—never biblical and never scientific.

Origin of the "Gap Theory"

These professing Christian geologists went far beyond the traditional understanding of a gap, inserting great ages into the historical gap. It is this mutated, bacterized misuse of the biblical gap that earned the name "Gap Theory" so as to demote it from a long-standing, well-accepted, biblical doctrine to an unsupported theory. Calling it a theory also equated it with the theory of evolution. No one called it a theory or a gap until it became the vehicle on which evolution would ride into the Christian coward's corner to be crowned Theistic Evolution—a weak Theos indeed.

The concept of a gap was not new, but the use of it to insert the Day Age Theory was new. Modern-day Young Earthers ignore the original biblical doctrine of a gap and pretend that the very concept of a gap was invented in the 1800s for the sole purpose of accommodating evolution. That is completely false, as the evidence shows.

Many who never liked the Bible in the first place are ready to fall at the feet of science and say "Amen. What wilt thou have me believe, lord?"

Orthodox View

During the 1800s and first half of the 1900s, Day Age gained ground among the weak in faith, but the concept of a gap continued to be the orthodox view among Bible believers. Major personalities like Spurgeon, Larkin, Scofield, Ironside, Arthur Pink, Barnhouse, Sauer, Criswell, Gabelein, Merrill Unger, and many others along with most Bible commentaries expressed belief in an old earth and universe. In 1917 with the publication of the Scofield Reference Bible, the age-old historical doctrine that was seldom spoken of became so common that thirty-seven years later in 1954, as stated earlier, noted theologian and writer Bernard Ramm, who did not believe in Spoken-Word Creation nor the traditional view of the Gap, wrote in *The Christian View of Science and Scripture*, "The gap theory has become the standard interpretation…"

Most Older Commentaries
Support the Creation Gap

None of the commentaries I have here in the office advocate for a young earth. **All assume an old earth**, and none sought to insert evolution into the Gap. They are: *The Bible Knowledge Commentary; A Commentary, Critical and Explanatory; The Wycliffe Bible Commentary; Jamieson, Fausset and Brown;* and *Bible Believer's Commentary.* I have others stored away in boxes, but it is not worth the time to free them from their graves. Long live digital books.

Beginning of the Young Earth Movement

During the latter part of the 1800s and early 1900s, while Bible-believing Christians held true to Gap Creationism, large segments of structured Christianity had fallen to some form of Progressive Creationism—that life forms developed gradually over billions of years by means of the guiding hand of the Almost Almighty.

In the 1950s and '60s, we heard about Theistic Evolutionists, but we dismissed them as neo-evangelicals, modernists, or liberals. They were of no concern because our paths never crossed. You would never see them at a revival meeting where we were singing "Power in the Blood." Nor did we run into them when ministering in prisons, rescue missions, or on the streets. They had no power to change lives, cast out devils, win the degenerate to faith in Christ, free the drug addict, or receive supernatural answers to prayers. If they cared about sin-sick individuals, they couldn't do anything for them other than establish some kind of a program based on psychology or drug therapy. Thus was born the Christian psychologist.

Progressive Creationists were mostly out of sight and out of mind, somewhere quietly sitting in big liberal churches with old names and tired histories, having no influence in the world. We called their seminaries "cemeteries." And if we met someone from one of the liberal churches, we immediately shared the gospel with them, knowing they had never been born again. Their God wasn't powerful enough to create by his spoken word alone.

In the 1960s the battle was NOT between creationism and evolution; it was between believing on Jesus Christ or not. Everyone knew that people who took the Bible at face value believed in Spoken Word Creation. And everyone else believed whatever they liked. It didn't much matter. It boiled down to two sides: those who believed the Bible and those who didn't. We understood it was a matter of informed faith on the one side and a secularist's worldview on the other. "Through faith we understand that the worlds were framed by the word of God, so that things which are seen were not made of things which do appear" (Hebrews 11:3).

A New Theory—Young Earthism

Then in 1961 **a new "ism"** was born. We call it new, not because no one had ever believed it before, but because it was to become known to the public and form **THE central doctrine in a new movement** that had never existed before, a belief that would bring people of various theological perspectives together with a zeal to evangelize the rest of Christianity and spread their new gospel to the rest of the world. Proponents prefer it to be called Scientific Creationism, but it is most accurately called the Young Earth Anti-Gap Theory. They do not hold an exclusive on belief in a six-day creation or a young earth. Their only exclusiveness is their Anti-Gap stance.

In 1961, John Whitcomb and Henry Morris coauthored *The Genesis Flood*. It was under their writings and others that followed that the ancient view of a gap between Genesis 1:1 and 1:3 was demoted to the "Gap Theory."

This new ism was on the opposite end of the pole from neo-evangelicalism or liberalism; it was a different form of hyper-orthodoxy, founded in science. It was indeed the seed of a modern trend that would fill the void left by a failure of faith in the mainline churches. Where faith was not enough to make Spoken Word Creationists out of vacillating believers, Scientific Creationism rushed in with an offer to "see and believe." As Christian psychology replaced the power of his resurrection Christian Scientism replaced belief in the words of God.

Meanwhile, in the minds and sermons of most Bible believers in the 1960s and '70s, the Gap Doctrine remained a peripheral issue that was of little concern unless one was teaching on the origin of angels and the Devil, or happened to be teaching Genesis or dispensationalism.

While this ism was gorging itself on science, growing fat with pride, most of us were unaware that the new movement would soon turn on traditional Christians with a theological vengeance. We were thankful for the work of Creation Science and its presentations on the complexities of nature and the absurdity of evolution. We read their books and utilized the information to extol our Creator and glory in the beauty of creation, but we just ignored their insistence upon a young earth, thinking that it must be a secondary issue that would go away if they ever got around to reading the Scripture. While we slept, comfortable in our historical foundations, scientists ran away with their Young Earth Theory through the eighties and nineties and down to the present.

We didn't take notice until their belief in a young universe seeped out into the general public, leaving the impression that their theory represented historical Bible doctrine. Then it became embarrassing, for they were dumbing down the Bible in the eyes of the public. We found evangelism more difficult, and we noticed their disciples being obnoxious with their limited knowledge of Young Earthism and their total lack of knowledge of the historical doctrine of Gap Creation. **They started using Young Earthism as a litmus test for orthodoxy, causing division among the brethren.**

The Final Straw

But the final straw that caused this author to take time out from teaching the Bible and attempting to reach the world for Christ to answer this heresy came when they started attacking our orthodoxy on major doctrines like the atoning work of Christ. We will address that subject in due course.

However, without a doubt, the greatest problem is the fact that evangelism is thwarted by Young Earth Scientism.

CHAPTER 4

YOUNG EARTH THEORISTS SPREAD FALSE AND MISLEADING INFORMATION

In his book *Unformed and Unfilled*, Weston Fields, a Gap denier, misrepresents the Gap view:

> "Not all gap theorists agree on the details of the theory, but the one unifying principle of all gap theorists is that Genesis 1:2 (1:1 in the case of the dependent clause view) records the ruin of a once-perfect earth, and a lengthy time-gap between the original creation and the restoration recorded in Genesis 1:3 to the end of the creation narrative. Other details of the theory are mere embellishments and are neither essential to the theory, nor universally held by all gap theorists." (p. 7)

He is NOT correct when he says that a **universally held**" is "**a lengthy gap.** be true, for if a Gap proponent assert crossed over from a Bible believer into must defend his position on the gro forces him to partner with evolutio his point. The Bible does not assert ruined earth due to Lucifer's fall. That could have occurred in a few years' time—even as little as a month. Granted, a number of Biblical Gapists yield to the geologists to assign the earth and universe any age they choose, for it is not relevant to Spoken Word Creation, but yielding the point is not the same as making it an essential part of one's belief in a gap.

You see, a Bible believer's reputation is not on the line when he yields science to the scientists and sticks with the Bible, but Creation Scientists are highly invested in their scientific theory of a young earth, so they get all bent out of shape and have launched a take-no-prisoners crusade. Leave us alone. We don't care. And stop providing a false definition of our position. That makes you part of the fake news network.

The Institute for Creation Research

The Institute for Creation Research (ICR) website misleads its readers with the following assertion.

> The Gap Theory "…arose when Christian leaders tried to accommodate the millions of years claimed by scientific research which was done by unsaved geologists, for fossil layers."[1]

Apparently ICR would rather not deal with the real origin of Gap Creationism, so they build a straw-man argument, poisoning the well for any who would drink from the fountain

---

1   http://www.icr.org/article/108/314

cient, biblically derived doctrine. They tend to impute methods to us, thinking we came to our Bible doctrines sed on current scientific trends. We do not try to accommodate funny theories like evolution. Give it a rest.

Answers in Genesis Defines What They Call "The Gap Theory"

"The idea is something like this: billions of years ago God created the space-mass-time universe. Then the geological ages took place over billions of years of earth history. The different forms of life developed that are now preserved in the fossil record. These life-forms represent those ages - the invertebrates of the Cambrian Period, the dinosaurs of the Cretaceous Period ... finally the mammals, birds and 'ape-men' of the Tertiary Period—just before the recent epoch."[1]

Huh? So that is what we believe? Is that what Augustine believed in the fourth century? Is that what Spurgeon believed? Is that what the king of England believed in the eleventh century? He has us old-time Bible believers and our historical doctrine confused with the views of a few secular scientists who know nothing of the Bible and never believed it anyway.

The Gap Theory—Robert W. Reed

"The Gap Theory (or Ruined-Reconstruction Theory) is an attempt by Christian theologians to harmonize the Genesis account of creation with the accepted geological ages. Even though many good

---

1   https://answersingenesis.org/genesis/gap-theory/the-gap-theory-an-idea-with-holes/

and godly Christians have been influenced by this teaching, it is still a compromised position to reconcile Moses and Darwin. The Gap Theory accommodates evolutionary teaching in that it allows millions of years for the age of the earth. It is only a theory which is unscientific, unscriptural, and unnecessary."[1]

Do those of us who have always believed in a gap get a say in what we believe and why? Did the Hebrew-reading Jews at the time of Christ "attempt to harmonize the Genesis account with the accepted geological ages" conceived eighteen hundred years later?

And if the Gap Fact "accommodates evolutionary teaching," **does the Bible accommodate Islam** since it claims Abraham as its father? **Does the book of Acts accommodate communists** who justify their doctrine on grounds the early church had all things in common? Does the Bible accommodate polygamists who point to scriptural examples? Has the Bible ever been used to accommodate slavery, war, racial prejudice, abuse of women, cruelty to children, the slaughter of heretics? The list is endless! Almost every evil in the world has found accommodation in the text of the Bible. Every Western heresy wants the Bible on its side. If we dismissed every Bible doctrine that has accommodated some evil or heresy, all that would be left is: "That which is crooked cannot be made straight: and that which is wanting cannot be numbered" (Ecclesiastes 1:15).

For Robert Reed to suggest that the accommodation argument carries any weight is demeaning to his readers. More than anything it demonstrates a dearth of evidence against

---

1   http://biblicaltruth.info/Articles/Gap%20Theory.htm

Gap Creationism and a desperation on the part of Young Earthism to shape the narrative before the public has opportunity to view the evidence.

Anti-Gap enthusiasts remind me of radical environmentalists in their singular zeal to promote this one idea and focus their entire life energies on it, severing relationships and forming new ones based on whether one agrees with them. In their passion to press the issue, they have trampled the truth and resorted to half-truths and invented facts. **"Fake news" is not restricted to the media.** Solomon said:

> "These six things doth the LORD hate…" and the six and seventh are "A false witness that speaketh lies, and **he that soweth discord among brethren.**" (Proverbs 6:16, 19)

Many Young Earth insisters are guilty of bearing "false witness," and by it they are sowing "discord among the brethren."

Here We Go Again

Jack Sofield makes another attempt at defining the Gap at Bible.org:

> "The gap theory exists for the purpose of allowing the geologic 'ages' as proposed by the assemblage of the geologic column."[1]

Bible.org does not quote a proponent of the Gap. Why allow a detractor to define it? They do not define the Gap as it was traditionally believed by Bible believers for thousands of years, nor as it continues to be believed by the average Christian today, but as it has been bastardized by unbelievers to make room for the geological ages supposedly required

---

1   https://bible.org/article/gap-theory-genesis-chapter-one

for evolution to occur. **It is dishonest to claim that it originated out of a desire to accommodate evolution**. Their falsehoods are an attempt to marginalize those who believe this historical doctrine.

Certainly in modern times Theistic Evolutionists have seized upon the historical Gap Doctrine to insert lengthy geological ages. But misuse and misapplication of a historical Bible doctrine is not grounds for rejecting the doctrine itself. If it were, then grace would be a false doctrine, for no biblical doctrine has been so systematically and institutionally misused as the doctrine of grace.

Kent Hovind on Thomas Chalmers

The booklet *The Gap Theory* by Kent Hovind and Stephen Lawwell attributes the origin of the "Gap Theory" as follows:

> "Thomas Chalmers (1780–1847), a notable Scottish theologian and first moderator of the Free Church of Scotland, is credited with being the first proponent of the gap theory. His proposal of the theory was first recorded in 1814 in one of his lectures at Edinburgh University. Prior to 1814, few theologians considered Genesis 1 as describing anything other than a normal 24-hour, six-day week." (p. 5)

Dr. Chalmers may be "**credited** with being the first proponent of the gap theory" by someone who has a vested interest in it not being supported by history, but the credit is not due. Dr. Chalmers references his source as the seventeenth-century Dutch Arminian theologian Simon Episcopius (1583–1643), writing more than two centuries before Darwin. And as already proven, there is a record of many others going all the way back to the early church and beyond who believed that Genesis 1:1 took place sometime before the six-day creation.

Note the slander in his characterization of Dr. Chalmers' position: "Prior to 1814, few theologians considered Genesis 1 as describing anything other than a normal 24-hour, six-day week." The writer implies that Chalmers believed the days of creation to be other than twenty-four hours, as if he were propagating The Day Age Theory, and that each day was millions or billions of years long so as to accommodate evolution. **That is pure slander**. Dr. Chalmers was a student of geology in a time when the apparent age of the earth was coming to the attention of academics. Being aware of the long-held doctrine of a gap of some undetermined length before the six days, Dr. Chalmers suggested that the Bible made provision for an old earth. He was not attempting to accommodate evolution. To the contrary, he was defending special creation by showing that the age of the earth has nothing to do with the timing of the six twenty-four hour days of creation as recorded in the Bible. He had no desire to leave a stumbling block in the way of skeptics as so many single-issue Christian scientists and their devotees are willing to do today.

John Whitcomb, Jr.

In the foreword to Weston Fields' book *Unformed and Unfilled*, John Whitcomb, Jr. carefully crafts his words to mislead, and he even dares to presume he knows the motives of Dr. Chalmers:

> "It was in 1814 that Dr. Thomas Chalmers of Edinburgh University first proposed what has since become known as the Gap Theory of Genesis 1:2. By this interpretation of the Bible, Dr. Chalmers

felt that he could make room for the vast expanse of time which the geologists of his day were demanding, and at the same time maintain a literal interpretation of the creation account. His views were further elaborated by George H. Pember *(Earth's Earliest Ages)* in 1876, and enormously popularized by a footnote in the Scofield Reference Bible (first edition, 1917)." (p. ix)

Whitcomb is shamefully misleading when he says, "Dr. Thomas Chalmers of Edinburgh University **first proposed** what has since become known as the Gap Theory..." The average reader who expects forthrightness in a Christian writer thinks he just read that the "Gap Theory" was unknown until 1844 when Chalmers "first proposed" it. But what Whitcomb craftily said was that Chalmers first proposed (*his* first proposal, not the first ever proposal) what **"became known"** as the Gap Theory. No one called it the "Gap Theory" until it accumulated detractors seeking to smear it with the label of a theory, thus equating it with the theory of evolution. They are employing a word association game designed to subtly influence the reader. It is indefensible to deceive the public with crafty wordsmithing.

Chalmers, in a long line of old-earth proponents throughout history, mentioned the concept of a gap without using the word, offering support by quoting a writer two centuries earlier; and later his belief in a two-stage creation is dubbed a gap and then a theory, so Chalmers is the author of the Gap Theory? Really? Something stinks on Sunday morning at Science Sunday School.

Wicked Wikipedia

At the time of this writing, Wikipedia lists a number of

men, including this author, as believing in "Progressive Creationism" otherwise known as Theistic Evolution.

"This book by Ramm was influential in the forma-tion of another alternative to gap creationism, that of progressive creationism, which found favour with more conservative members of the American Sci-entific Affiliation (a fellowship of scientists who are Christians), with the more modernist wing of that fellowship favouring theistic evolution.

Religious proponents of this form of creationism have included Oral Roberts, Cyrus I. Scofield, Harry Rimmer, Jimmy Swaggart, G. H. Pember, L. Allen Higley, Arthur Pink, Peter Ruckman, Finis Jennings Dake, Chuck Missler, E. W. Bullinger, Donald Grey Barnhouse, Herbert W. Armstrong, Garner Ted Armstrong, **Michael Pearl** and Clar-ence Larkin."[1]

None of the men listed in Wikipedia are guilty of such an egregious error—certainly not Michael Pearl. I know, because I have read everything he has written and I sleep with his wife.

Are Young Earth Theorists so insecure in their position that they must misrepresent the historical doctrine to render it vulnerable to attack and then boldly lie about the men who continue to hold to Gap Creationism? The Young Earth Theorists who put this in Wikipedia violated the ninth commandment: "Thou shalt not bear false witness against thy neighbor."

I predict Young Earthism will become an Old Wasum' as the public becomes weary with the theory and adherents become better informed.

---

1   https://en.wikipedia.org/wiki/Gap_creationism

Objective Observer

Scientific Young Earthers are adept at smearing traditional Gap advocates with the suggestion or outright accusation of compromising with the evolutionary geologists. Tom McIver, advocating for a purely scientific approach—not a friend of Creationists of any stripe—makes an observation from one on the outside observing the Gap controversy:

> "Gap theory advocates, by this maneuver, are able to reconcile the scientific evidence for an old Earth and universe and for life itself. They, just as much as the young-Earth creationists, reject evolution; to them, the re-creation six thousand or so years ago was not entirely ex nihilo (although humans may have been created out of nothing) but was certainly by divine fiat. Therefore, although they differ markedly from "strict" creationists regarding the age of Earth, their anti-evolution attitudes and arguments are virtually identical." (*"Formless and Void,"* p. 2)

Without any skin in the game, this objective observer recognizes what the Young Earth Theorists are unwilling to admit: we Pre-Six-Day Creationists always have been and remain Spoken Word Creationists. Why do we not receive the same honest courtesy from Christian Scientists?

Are They Lying through Their Teeth?

No, they are lying through their truth. To speak the truth and impart a falsehood is a learned craft, highly developed in the political arena and in modern media. Yet we observe respected men of purported integrity unashamedly asserting patently false statements about the antiquity and nature of the pre-six-day creation. What are they thinking? We must turn to the writings of an unbelieving evolutionist to discover the **mental gymnastics that allow them to assert a false-hood while believing they are speaking the truth**.

Tom McIver, a critic of all forms of Spoken Word Creation, unwittingly reveals how one can be familiar with the evidence and yet deny that the Gap Doctrine was common throughout church history. Young Earth Theorists adopt this same method of reasoning.

> "Claims that there were gap theory proponents prior to the rise of modern geology probably **distort the intent of these early writers and commentators**, though they **may have believed in a preexistent chaos** or a period of preparation before the six-day creation." (*"Formless and Void"*)

He said **"they may have believed in a preexisting chaos."** There is no "may have believed." They said they did. When we submit ten bold examples, he says we are probably distorting **"the intent of these early writers."** According to the All Discerning One, they didn't intend to be saying what they said. They said it but they meant to be saying something else, something he would rather they said, that the Bible teaches the earth and universe were created just six thousand years ago. Why does he want them to say that when he doesn't believe it? Because he finds it very easy to dismiss Young Earthism and by doing so he dismisses the Bible as factual. For it is not so easy for the geologists to dismiss the Bible if it makes allowance for an old earth and universe. So he dismisses the argument for Gap Creationism by denying the evidence.

His logic goes like this.

- It is a fact that the universe is older than six thousand years.

- The Bible teaches it is just six thousand years old.
- Therefore the Bible is not factual.

Here is the reality he seeks to avoid:

- It is a fact that the universe is older than six thousand years.
- The Bible teaches that it is older than six thousand years.
- Therefore the Bible is correct on that point.

He would then have to come up with another argument against the Bible and defend evolution on the grounds of science alone. As it is, he is able to shut down the debate before it even gets to the science. Apparently neither the evolutionists nor the Young Earth Scientists want to debate evolution on the grounds of science alone.

Note that he reluctantly admitted that "early writers and commentators" did write of a **"preexistent chaos"** before the six days of creation. Today we call that a Gap—for anyone interested in the facts.

The Crux of the Construct

But this advocate of evolution (above) has revealed a behind-the-scenes trick shared by evolutionists and Young Earthers alike. By reserving the right to define the "Gap Theory" in a narrow way, they can say it didn't exist until it was commandeered to harmonize the Bible with evolution. And since it is then associated with the *theory* of evolution, it too is a theory. So in their thinking the "Gap Theory" did not exist until the nineteenth century when it was used by some to accommodate the geological ages. By defining the Gap in this convoluted manner, Young Earthers are able to exclude many ancient commentaries from the list of witnesses because they didn't utilize the Gap to accommodate geological ages. That would be like Dale Mulder of A&W claiming there were no hamburgers until 1963 when he started putting cheese and bacon on them. Young Earthism may like a Gap with evolution smeared on it, but the rest of us believed it a long time before anyone thought to decorate it with Darwin dip.

Well I have news for McIver and all Young Earthers who manipulate the history in this manner: we still believe what the writers of old believed. It is simple. The Bible clearly reveals that the first day of creation recorded in Genesis 1:3 was on an earth that already existed for some undetermined length of time. Young Earth Theorists want to stuff us into their preconceived mold so as to accommodate their agenda through demonizing the historical Gap Doctrine as being complicit with evolution.

They set up an "either/or" situation. Either you are a Creationist believing in a young earth or you are a liberal, turncoat, new-evangelical, modernist, evolution-accommodating Gap Theory proponent. We don't fit in their agenda and we won't wear their label.

I say to the Young Earth Theorists, speak for yourselves and let us define what we believe. Stop deceiving the public with your word games. And **stop selecting come-lately extremist views of the Gap as a representation of the historical doctrine**. You are lying through your truth when you privately define the Gap Doctrine according to late and limited use and then earnestly assert that the Gap (as you define it) did not exist until the nineteenth century.

Christians who have accepted your Young Earthism will be shocked to learn of your deliberate deception. They will feel used, as they should. You should have known better than to perpetuate a falsehood when the facts were so readily available.

Institute for Creation Research

Bible.org utilizes a quote by Weston W. Fields, an opponent of the Gap, to define the "Gap Theory."

> "The gap theory is not of recent origin but can be traced back to the early 19th century when the new discipline of geology was breaking upon the scientific scene… the gap theory, along with other accommodation theories, is an attempt to reconcile a great age for the earth, as presented by geologists, with the relatively young age as deduced from the Biblical record."[1]

What he should have said is the **Gap Theory "can be traced back to the early 19th century when"** detractors decided to call a millenniums-old belief a **theory.**

But the big falsehood is the last phrase he slipped in, "…**relatively young age as deduced from the Biblical record.**" His deduction that the earth is young does not come from any biblical record; it comes from someone's scientific opinion. Show me one verse that indicates the heaven and earth are young. Just one. A little one will do. No reference to scientific opinion. Just a verse.

Christiananswers.net

How could a writer be so ignorant as the following? Or maybe we should ask, how could a writer be so dishonest?

> "Western Bible commentaries written before the 18th century, and before the belief in a long age for the Earth became popular, knew nothing of any gap between Genesis 1:1 and Genesis 1:2. Certainly some commentaries proposed intervals of various

---

1   https://bible.org/article/gap-theory-genesis-chapter-one

lengths of time for reasons relating to Satan's fall, but none proposed a 'ruin-reconstruction' situation, or pre-Adamite world.[1]

"Western Bible commentaries… knew nothing of any gap"? **Seriously**? There were many, and you have read a number of them. Remember, King Edgar of England (943–975) expressed belief in a gap. At that time, anyone WEST of England was painting pictures of buffalo on their teepees. The only gap they knew was the Grand Canyon.

Notice the subtlety in the qualifier "**Western Bible commentaries**." What about Eastern, like the birthplace of all Scripture, the place where writing was developed, paper was invented, math was discovered, the first books were published, the early church existed—what about them? Does their understanding not count? Why just "Western"? The ancient Hebrews interpreted the Hebrew Bible as indicating a gap. Did this naysayer know that the original Aramaic Bible assumed a gap? What about the early Egyptian commentaries and other writers that were not "Western"? Does an idea not exist until it is assimilated by Westerners? Did advanced math not exist until the Renaissance when Westerners imported it from the East? Did tomatoes not exist until the Italians made tomato paste? It is bad enough to have bad logic, but when bad logic is based on false premises, it is not just bad logic; it's lying, illogical lunacy.

But he does admit that "**some commentaries proposed intervals of various lengths of time…**" Any length of time is a gap, is it not? So even with his limited historical perspective he acknowledges the antiquity of the Creation Gap. He knows better; it is just better for his argument if his imagination is true.

---

1   https://christiananswers.net/q-aig/aig-c003.html

If Young Earthists were transparent with the evidence, informing their readers of early acceptance of the Gap, they could then argue that proponents of the Gap were incorrect and then present their reasons why; but to mislead with the evidence so as to dismiss the subject before one hears from the witnesses is downright crooked to the core.

Do you see the verbal gymnastics Christiananswers.net performs? **They are saying the "Gap Theory" didn't exist until someone used it to accommodate evolution.** That is like saying wheat didn't exist until someone baked it into a tooth-decaying Hostess Twinkie, and that because it has been baked into a Twinkie, wheat is now bad. You may be gluten intolerant and Gap intolerant, but some of us are not, and we still eat whole wheat bread and believe in Gap Creationism just like the early church.

Tom McIver on Fields

Tom McIver quotes Weston Fields as suggesting a date for the Gap earlier than Chalmers.

> "According to Fields, the first genuine statements of the gap theory were proposed in 1776 by J. C. Rosenmuller and in 1791 by J. A. Dathe."
> (*"Formless and Void,"* p. 6)

At least this author is aware of what Kent Hovind missed: that Chalmers was not the first to believe in the Gap.

Note the careful wording: "**the first genuine statements of the gap theory.**" Those who read no further than modern books put out by Creation Scientists are led to believe in a recent origin for the Gap, but, knowing that some of us may be paying attention and may charge him with witness tampering, he qualifies his statement of its age with the word "**genuine**." Fields has taken it upon himself to make a judgment as to what constitutes a "genuine" Gap Doctrine. He, as others, are looking at extreme uses of the Gap and christening them as genuine. Why? They are building straw men that are easy to knock down with their empty-fisted arguments. Shame, shame.

Tom McIver

We are examining how those who know of the many ancient records of a gap can boldly assert that it is a new theory. Tom McIver, an opponent of the Gap, reveals their mental gymnastics and word games:

> "Fields denied Custance's claim of early support
> for the gap theory, arguing that some of the an-
> cient commentators perhaps supposed there was
> an interval between Genesis 1:1 and 1:2 but that
> none of them ever posited a gap of vast ages with a
> "ruin-and-reconstruction" scenario."
> (*"Formless and Void,"* p. 6)

You will read Young Earthists' literature stating emphatically that Fields answered Custance's arguments for early belief in the Gap. Fields answered it by defining the Gap Theory as a belief accommodating the geological age theory in support of evolution. The ancient testimonies speak for themselves. **One cannot build an argument by shifting definitions.**

> "The gap theory became a respectable means of rec-
> onciliation due in large part to Chalmers' prestigious
> advocacy. He may well be the actual inventor of the
> gap theory as well, at least in the form in which it is
> known today." (*"Formless and Void,"* p. 6)

His reasoning is that because the ancient writers did not flesh out the Gap Doctrine in exactly the same way as do some modern proponents who are attempting to answer the charges of geologists, its modern application makes it a new doctrine. When you put aftermarket parts on an old car, do you date the car's origin to the moment of modification? And if the aftermarket parts detract from the original automobile, do you hold the auto manufacturer responsible? You would if you were highly invested in the Young Car Theory.

If Young Earthers were upfront with their argument and forthrightly consented that the ancients did indeed believe in a gap of some **undetermined** length between the chaotic earth and the six days of creation, then they could proceed to honestly argue that the old doctrine has been misused in modern times to make the Bible compliant with geology. And that would then be a matter for honest discussion. But with their subtly worded denials, they have left the public believing a lie with hopes of ending the conversation before it gets started.

Know that we proponents of the historical Gap sit here unscathed by their straw-men arguments. They have missed the mark by attacking something on which they placed our name. It is like burning an effigy: we resent the inference but we don't feel the heat, and we are still standing even as the fire of criticism burns. Yet like the three Hebrew children, we do not even have the smell of fire on us.

CHAPTER 5

HISTORY OF SATAN

What is so important about the historical, biblical doctrine of a gap that it would provoke Satan to slander it at this late hour—and, of all things, by science-worshiping Christians? The Gap Doctrine plays a major role in God's eternal program. Taking it into account is the only way to make sense of the biblical narrative, the human plight, and Satan's campaign against the world. Without including the Gap in our equation, Satan looks irrationally obsessive as he seeks to sabotage God's program on earth. And irrational he is not.

The First Sons of God

The first and original sons of God were angels. The term "sons of God" is found in the Old Testament just six times, and five are in reference to angels (Genesis 6:2, 4; Job 1:6; 2:1; 38:7). The sixth is in reference to Jesus Christ (Daniel 3:25). Adam is called the son of God in Luke 3:38, but no other human is called a son of God until Jesus shows up. The angels were God's first attempt at establishing a kingdom here on earth. It was not a failure, as it may appear, for the fall of these first sons of God set the stage for a moral conflict that would provide the boot camp necessary to perfect the new sons of God found in Adam's race. More about this later.

The angels already existed before the earth was created, for they were present and rejoicing when the foundations of the earth were laid. The proof text is undeniable. God humbles Job by asking him a question he cannot answer, for the events occurred before the six days of recreation.

> **Job 38:4** Where wast thou when **I laid the foundations of the earth**? declare, if thou hast understanding.
> **5** Who hath laid the measures thereof, if thou knowest? or who hath stretched the line upon it?
> **6** Whereupon are the foundations thereof fastened? or who laid the corner stone thereof;
> **7** When the morning stars sang together, and all the sons of God shouted for joy?

The above passage in Job cannot be identified with the six days of creation in the first chapter of Genesis, for chapter one briefly acknowledges God as the creator, but the six days of creation begin with an assumption of the earth already existing in a state of judgment—"without form and void." God said the angels were present and shouting for joy when he **laid the foundations**—something you do before construction can begin.

God called those first angelic beings "**sons of God**," and he placed them on his new planet in a place called Eden (Ezekiel 28:13). Perhaps that is why they stood by and sang together, occasionally breaking out into a shout of joy, as they anticipated the completion of their new home.

Therefore, since the sons of God were present when the foundations of the earth were being laid, Bible students throughout history have accurately concluded that Lucifer and the angels, and their fall, predate the creation of the earth.

History of Lucifer and the Angels

Before his rebellion, Lucifer was an anointed cherub who covered the throne of God (Ezekiel 28:14) perfect in all his ways (Ezekiel 28:15). Similar creatures who didn't rebel still surround the throne. Revelation 4:7–9 describes their appearance and their role before God.

Before his sin, for a time Lucifer dwelt in the place called Eden—not the garden in which Adam dwelt (Ezekiel 28:13). Eden is the region stretching from the rivers of Iraq and Turkey, including the western edge of Iran, Syria, Kuwait, part of Egypt, and up the coast of the Mediterranean through Israel and Lebanon to southern Turkey (see Genesis 2:10–14, 4:16; Amos 1:5; Ezekiel 27:23; Isaiah 37:12 for a description of the geography.). It is the land God gave later to Israel on the re-created earth. "God planted a garden eastward in Eden" (Genesis 2:8) where he placed Adam. It is obvious that God not only selected this planet as home for his kingdom, he also selected the particular region, encompassing Jerusalem.

Lucifer was especially beautiful and glorious. He was adorned with nine precious stones laid in gold (Ezekiel 28:13), probably like the high priests of Israel (Exodus 28:15–21). Apparently, as strange as it sounds, he was "created" with the capacity to make music within his own body, possessing both percussion ("tabrets") and wind instruments ("pipes") as part of his physical structure (Isaiah 14:11). He was a walking, reasoning, flying pipe organ. With his high status, beauty, wisdom, and musical ability, he may have been the worship and praise leader around the throne, for four living creatures, one of whom sports his ox face, continue in that role (Revelation 5:6–14).

His physical appearance was striking. The prophet Ezekiel describes "living creatures" he saw in a vision (Ezekiel 1:5–14). They have the profile of a man, shiny like polished brass, with feet like a calf's foot, cloven and straight, and four wings, probably mammal wings like a bat, not feathers as depicted in classical art. Each has four faces, "they four had the face of a **man**, and the face of a **lion,** on the right side: and they four had the face of an **ox** on the left side; they four also had the face of an **eagle**" (Ezekiel 1:10). There are eyes strategically located in various places about their bodies. Their hands are under their wings, probably like a bat's hands. They move with the speed and flash of lightning as they support the throne of God. In the book of Revelation they are found to surround the throne with constant praise (Revelation 4:7–9).

By doing a little detective work we are able to identify the face of a cherub—Lucifer's face. In 1:10, Ezekiel lists the four faces as (1) man, (2) lion, (3) ox, and (4) eagle. And then in 10:14 he lists them again but exchanges the word *ox* for the word *cherub*. Instead of man, lion, **ox**, and eagle, it is man, lion, **cherub**, and eagle. Thus we are told that a cherub has the face of an ox. Lucifer's original face is that of an ox. Is it any wonder that the most commonly worshiped god of the ancient world was an ox or calf? Satan inspired Israel to construct a golden calf (burnished brass in color like the living creatures). As a nation they fell back into Baal worship from time to time. Baal was in the image of a bull, or ox. Satan is proud of his original appearance and seeks recognition through the idols men erect. Thus India worships the many oxen that freely roam the streets. Spain has always had its bulls sacrificed by matadors while the crowd cheers. Mexico and other countries have "the running of the bulls." Satan, formerly Lucifer, "anointed cherub," sporting the face of an ox, loves his image and seeks its promotion. The love of money, being the root of all evil (1 Timothy 6:10), and Satan being the author of all evil and guilty of a sin involving merchandising (Ezekiel 28:16), he loves to hear Wall Street use the phrase "bull market."

Discontent with his assignment on the original earth and lusting after additional glory, in an act of rebellion Lucifer ascended to heaven, expecting to be like the Most High and to establish his throne on the mountain of God (Isaiah 14:13). He lied to the angels, seducing one-third of them (Revelation 12:4) to follow him in a revolutionary uprising where he committed murder, becoming the first murderer, and the first sinner, and the father of all lies.

> "Ye are of your father the devil, and the lusts of
> your father ye will do. He was a murderer from
> the beginning, and abode not in the truth, because
> there is no truth in him. When he speaketh a lie, he
> speaketh of his own: for he is a liar, and the father
> of it." (John 8:44)

In response to Lucifer's sin, God cast him down to the earth and, consistent with the pattern we see in the second and third judgments, the earth was cursed (Isaiah 14:12; Ezekiel 28:18).

Genesis 1:2 And the earth was without form, and void; and darkness was upon the face of the deep. And the Spirit of God moved upon the face of the waters.

Jeremiah 4:23 I beheld the earth, and, lo, it was **without form, and void**; and the heavens, and they had no light *[cannot be Noah's flood]*.
24 I beheld the mountains, and, lo, they trembled, and all the hills moved lightly.
25 I beheld, and, lo, there was **no man** *[cannot be the tribulation nor Noah's flood]*, and all the birds of the heavens were fled.
26 I beheld, and, lo, the fruitful place was a wilderness, and all the cities thereof were broken down at the presence of the LORD, and by his fierce anger.

During Noah's flood, the cities and fruitful places would not be visible, and after the flood when the waters receded, it could not be said that it was formless and void and that there was no light. Clearly, this is a description of the earth in Genesis 1:2 before the recreation.

Later the earth was found to be **without form and void** (Genesis 1:2), covered with **water** (Psalm 32:7; Genesis 1:2), shrouded in thick **darkness** (Job 38:9). Apparently it was cursed as a result of Lucifer's sin just as it was cursed when Adam sinned and again during the days of Noah, and will be cursed once more at the end of the Millennium when it will be destroyed and a new earth created (Revelation 21:1). That demonstrates a pattern with God. The earth will experience four destructions and four renewals, if you count the Tribulation and Millennium as one of them: (1) the original creation before the six days, (2) Noah's judgment, (3) the Tribulation and Millennium (Isaiah 2:1–3), and (4) the end of the Millennium when a new heaven and earth are created (Revelation 20–21). God's march to the Kingdom of Heaven was sovereignly planned and will be timely executed.

Lucifer Was the First Sinner, Having Sinned before Adam and Eve

Ezekiel 28:15 Thou wast perfect in thy ways from the day that thou wast created, till iniquity was found in thee.

John 8:44 Ye are of your father the devil, and the lusts of your father ye will do. He was a **murderer from the beginning**, and abode not in the truth, because there is no truth in him. When he speaketh a lie, he speaketh of his own: for he is a liar, and the father of it.

Lucifer, Now Called the Devil and Satan, Still Has Access to Heaven (Revelation 20:10).

Job 1:6 Now there was a day when the sons of God came to present themselves before the LORD, and Satan came also among them.

His mission now is to defeat the work of God in the new sons of God (1 Peter 5:7–8). At this present time the Devil and his many devils have established themselves as our adversaries, seeking to devour every believer (1 Peter 5:8). It is a wrestling match unto death that requires preparation and defensive armor as well as the offensive weapon of an infallible book of promises (Ephesians 6:10–18).

Revelation 12:10 And I heard a loud voice saying in heaven, Now is come salvation, and strength, and the kingdom of our God, and the power of his

Christ: for the accuser of our brethren is cast down,
which accused them before our God day and night.
11 And they overcame him by the blood of the
Lamb, and by the word of their testimony; and they
loved not their lives unto the death.

At the beginning of the millennial reign of Christ, Satan will
be cast out of heaven for good, back down to earth where he
will be confined to the bottomless pit for a thousand years,
after which he will be released to perform one last temptation by deceiving the nations into attempting what he failed
to do—to come against the throne of God in an attempt
to overthrow the government of God and reign in his place
(Revelation 12:3–4; 20:1–10).

> **Revelation 12:9** And the great dragon was cast out,
> that old serpent, called the Devil, and Satan, which
> deceiveth the whole world: he was cast out into the
> earth, and his angels were cast out with him.

At the end of the Millennium, Satan will be loosed from his
prison and will immediately continue his campaign against
the Kingdom of Heaven. He will "**go out to deceive the
nations which are in the four quarters of the earth… to
gather them together to battle**" (Revelation 20:710)
against the kingdom. But without so much as a warning or
a ceremony, he and the forces that join him will be swiftly
destroyed by fire from heaven (Revelation 20:9). Afterward
the saints of God pass judgment upon him (1 Corinthians
6:1) and he will be cast into the Lake of Fire (Revelation
20:14) where he will be **"tormented day and night for ever
and ever"** (Revelation 20:10).

We Can Conclude

From the Bible text it is indisputable that Lucifer and the angels (sons of God) were created before the earth, dwelt on the earth, and ascended up to heaven in rebellion; Satan lied and committed murder in the beginning, was cast down to the earth, and was present in the garden as a disembodied spirit shortly after Adam and Eve were created.

Therefore, before Adam and Eve sinned, there was a sinner already present in the atmosphere around the earth (Ephesians 2:2). And, foremost, before Adam and Eve sinned and received the penalty of death, Lucifer had already committed murder as part of his original sin. Eve was the first human sinner (1 Timothy 2:14) on the newly re-created planet but not the first sinner. Adam and Eve brought death upon the human race, but death itself had already occurred upon the planet to Lucifer and the sinning angels (Psalm 82:6–7). We know that one of Adam's sons murdered the other, so the murder committed in the beginning by Satan, the first murderer, had to have occurred before Cain killed Abel. And we know it was not a human he killed.

CHAPTER **6**

GOD'S KINGDOM PROGRAM

Two Different Kingdoms

The Gap is best understood in connection with the Kingdom of Heaven—not the Kingdom of God, for the pre-adamic earth was the original Kingdom of Heaven with angels and cherubim as subjects of the kingdom and the earth and stars as their domain (Ephesians 2:2; Revelation 6:13; 9:1; 12:4).

The Kingdom of God and the Kingdom of Heaven are not the same place, do not have the same inhabitants nor the same kings, and they serve different purposes—though they do have a number of things in common, and under the right circumstances can coexist in harmony, which they should, and eventually will. The Kingdom of God is the spiritual reign of God over the hearts of men and angels and any other creature unknown to us anywhere in the universe or beyond in heaven or in hell (Psalm 139:6). The Kingdom of God is everywhere hearts and spirit are in fellowship with God.

Jesus said, "The kingdom of God **cometh not with observation**: Neither shall they say, Lo here! or, lo there! for, behold, **the kingdom of God is within you**" (Luke 17:20–21). You enter the Kingdom of God by being born again—coming into favor with God (John 3:3–5).

The Kingdom of Heaven

The Kingdom of Heaven is a physical, visible kingdom in the tangible heavens, the place where spaceships fly and stars twinkle. Presently the Kingdom of Heaven is only on earth and in the space station located on the outer edge of the first heavens, but if we were to colonize Mars, it would be there as well under the flag of the sponsoring country.

Originally the Kingdom of Heaven was given to Lucifer—the first temporal son of God. He fell and the kingdom domain was made "without form and void" (Jeremiah 4:23; Isaiah 14:14). God reestablished the kingdom under a new son of God (Hebrews 2:5–8), but Adam surrendered it to the former ruler—Satan—making him "the god of this world" (2 Corinthians 4:4).

The Bible, as well as secular history, is the story of different factions seeking to control the kingdom. It contains sinners and devils alike (Matthew 13:41). The Kingdom of Heaven can be taken by force of arms (Matthew 11:12), because it is an actual kingdom in the heavens (which include earth).

The modern, progressive, Christian worship movement speaks much about "the kingdom" with a totally skewed understanding of what it is. Jehovah's Witnesses think they meet in a Kingdom Hall. The Mormons think their church is the one and only Kingdom of Heaven. The Roman Catholic Church thinks it is the sole representative of the Kingdom of Heaven.

Thy Kingdom Come

Jesus acknowledged Satan's kingdom (Matthew 12:26). From time to time Satan shares the kingdom with men like Hitler and Stalin, but in the end the Kingdom of God will subdue the usurpers of the Kingdom of Heaven by an overpowering act of violence (Matthew 11:12; Revelation 11:15) with a war to end all wars at the end of the Great Tribulation; and the Kingdom of Heaven will come as was meant to be, and the will of God will be done on earth as it is in heaven (Matthew 6:10). Then the meek "shall inherit the earth" (Matthew 5:5) while King Jesus reigns (Isaiah 9:7) over the kingdom. In that one-thousand-year period, the Kingdom of God will merge with the Kingdom of Heaven and become Christ's Kingdom until the end of the Millennium, at which time all kingdoms will become the Father's Kingdom (Revelation 12:10; 1 Corinthians 15:24–28). See my book *Eight Kingdoms* for a detailed account of the biblical kingdoms.

The New Testament narrative opens with "In those days came John the Baptist, preaching in the wilderness of Judaea, And saying, Repent ye: **for the kingdom of heaven is at hand**" (Matthew 3:1–2). Jesus came with the same kingdom message: "From that time Jesus began to preach, and to say, Repent: **for the kingdom of heaven is at hand**" (Matthew 4:17). They were offering the kingdom promised to Israel. The main body of Jesus' parables is called, "the **kingdom** parables," for all of them begin with "The kingdom of heaven is like unto…" (Matthew 13).

What Does All This Have to Do with a Gap?

What does all of this have to do with the Gap? To disregard the former kingdom that existed on this earth wherein Lucifer played a major role is to castigate the scriptural doctrine of the Kingdom of Heaven. To remove the Gap from Bible history is to leave a glaring hole in God's kingdom program.

Lucifer made his decision to rebel while residing in the original Kingdom of Heaven located on this earth (Isaiah 14:14). In Scripture we see a clear pattern repeated all the way to the end of the Millennium. The Gap is a perfect fit in the tapestry of God's program, and it is essential to understanding the biblical narrative. To remove the Gap is like beginning in the middle of a movie after the characters have been introduced and the reasons for the drama revealed. You are left wondering, what is this story all about? What is the end-goal of this evil antagonist? Why the compelling animosity? As is common in many books, the background information is not given in the first chapter. It is a mystery that is leaked to the reader through clues a little at a time as needed to reveal motivations and suggest outcomes.

The Bible begins with an assumption of some former act of destruction and with an evil nemesis lurking in our story, attempting to thwart the will of the lead character. In due course we discover that he is one of the gods (Psalm 82:6) knowing good and evil (Genesis 3:5), that he is a shrewd liar and deceiver (Genesis 3:1–13), and that his deceptions appeared to lead to the ruin of God's program to inaugurate a righteous kingdom. Those who dismiss the Gap dismiss the history of Satan and do violence to the kingdom message, rendering biblical history unfathomable.

Young Earthism began as a movement among Calvinists, Henry Morris being the founder of the movement. Most of the big names supporting it today are Calvinists, with exceptions such as Ken Ham, whom they denigrate for his theology. Calvinists have continued with the Roman

Catholic approach of allegorizing Scripture and denying dispensationalism. They are not endowed with a historical understanding of God's great plan of the ages, so they do not appreciate the significance of their dismissal of so vital a part of the big picture.

CHAPTER 7

SCRIPTURE

"In the beginning God created the heaven and the earth."
The phrase "in the beginning" cannot be applied to the six days because verse two severs verse three from the beginning event with the connective sequencer *And*.

"And the earth was without form, and void; and darkness was upon the face of the deep."
This description has always been understood by ancient Hebrew writers to speak of degeneration and ruin—not creation. To circumvent getting in the weeds on a discussion of Hebrew, I will avoid arguing that the word *was* was understood by ancient Hebrews to carry the meaning of "became." We need not go there to establish the facts. The English reader can always rely upon the Authorized Version to interpret its own words and phrases. Of course that is not true of the more than two hundred corrupt commercial versions produced in the last 134 years, beginning with the

Revised Version of 1885. So a simple concordance search in your favorite King James Bible program turns up a rather fascinating word match.

The prophet Jeremiah, noted for his end-time prophecies of judgment, utilized the identical phrase in pronouncing judgment upon the land of Israel. Most Bible-believing commentators believe verses 23–26 of chapter 4 is a reference to the former desolation of the earth in Genesis 1:2, for it is a very common practice for the prophets to utilize former judgments to illustrate coming judgments.

Note, the context of the entire passage is destruction and ruin.

Jeremiah 4:20 Destruction upon destruction is cried; for the whole land is *[present tense]* **spoiled:** suddenly are my tents spoiled, and my curtains in a moment.

The following four verses are in the past tense, and are a reference to the earlier destruction of Genesis 1:2.

23 I beheld *[past tense]* the earth, and, lo, it was *[past tense]* **without form, and void**; and the heavens, and **they had no light**.
24 I beheld *[past tense]* the mountains, and, lo, **they trembled**, and all the hills moved lightly.
25 I beheld, and, lo, there was **no man**, and all the birds of the **heavens were fled**.
26 I beheld, and, lo, the **fruitful place was a wilderness**, and all the cities thereof were *[past tense]* **broken down** at the presence of the LORD, and by his **fierce anger**.

Jeremiah returns to the future tense to address the coming plight of Israel.

> **27** For thus hath the LORD said, The whole land
> **shall be** *[future]* desolate; yet will I not make a full
> end. *[There was a full end in the above four verses]*
> **28** For this shall *[future tense]* the earth mourn, and
> the heavens above be black: because I have spoken
> it, I have purposed it, and will not repent, neither
> will I turn back from it.

Earlier in verse 25 Jeremiah characterized the judgment as
resulting in "**no man**" and no **birds** on the earth, conditions
that did not occur in Israel's judgment and will not occur
during the Tribulation, for the Tribulation ends with the
birds of the air eating the flesh of the damned (Revelation
19:17–18). But the judgment upon Israel will not result in
the extinguishing of all human and bird life. It will result in
the evacuation of the population of the city of Jerusalem only.

> **29** The whole city shall flee for the noise of the
> horsemen and bowmen; they shall go into thickets,
> and climb up upon the rocks: every city shall be
> forsaken, and not a man dwell therein.

It is difficult to believe in the objectivity of anyone who
would interpret verses 23–26 as anything other than conditions prior to the six days.

Out of the Dead Weeds

Since the above passage in Jeremiah has long been referenced
as support for the Gap Doctrine, Young Earth Theorists have
developed a novel interpretation that Jeremiah is not speaking
of former events when he interrupts his future prophecy to
inject four verses in the past tense. So we may find ourselves
in the weeds debating over a point that is irrelevant to our
purpose here, which is simply to gain an understanding of
the phrase "without form and void." So for the moment, we

will concede that Jeremiah made a mistake in using the past tense and that the conditions described are of the future tribulation only. So, given the context of the phrase, what does it mean? We learn that the "formless and void" state is not something God created; it is the result of judgement.

Everything God created during the six days is said to be "very good." But, as in Jeremiah 4, there was nothing good about verse two—"without form, and void; and darkness upon the face of the deep." That is a negative state resulting from judgment.

"...and darkness was upon the face of the deep."
Again the whole point of creation was to make good things. If you run a concordance search on the word darkness, you will discover its negative connotation all the way through the Bible.

> **Genesis 15:12** And when the sun was going down, a deep sleep fell upon Abram; and, lo, an **horror of great darkness** fell upon him.

> **Exodus 10:21** And the LORD said unto Moses, Stretch out thine hand toward heaven, that there may be **darkness over the land of Egypt**, even **darkness** which may be felt.

> **Job 3:4** Let that day be darkness; let not God regard it from above, neither let the light shine upon it.
> **5** Let **darkness and the shadow of death** stain it; let a cloud dwell upon it; let the blackness of the day terrify it.
> **6** As for that night, let darkness seize upon it; let it not be joined unto the days of the year, let it not come into the number of the months.

Luke 11:34 The light of the body is the eye: therefore when thine eye is single, thy whole body also is full of light; but **when thine eye is evil, thy body also is full of darkness**.
35 Take heed therefore that the light which is in thee be not darkness.

John 1:3 All things were made by him; and without him was not any thing made that was made.
4 In him was life; and the life was the light of men.
5 And the **light shineth in darkness**; and the darkness comprehended it not.

John 3:19 And this is the condemnation, that light is come into the world, and men **loved darkness** rather than light, **because their deeds were evil**.

John 12:46 I am come a light into the world, that whosoever believeth on me should **not abide in darkness**.

1 John 1:5 This then is the message which we have heard of him, and declare unto you, that God is light, and **in him is no darkness at all**.

Allowing the Bible to define its terms, it is clear that the darkness of Genesis 1:2 is a negative state resulting from something unholy. How could God create darkness and call it good? He didn't.

"And the Spirit of God moved upon the face of the waters."
This phrase foreshadows God's preparation to do something about this negative state. Note that the Spirit of God moves in darkness upon the face of the waters which completely cover the earth. At what point in the six days did this occur?

The very first act is to remove the darkness with light. It is untenable that the moment described should ever exist in the six days. It is clearly describing conditions prior to the first day when light dispels the darkness.

The Six Days

A simple diagram of the six days of creation reveals that the original creation of heaven and earth was not part of the six days. Each of the six days of creation begin with the statement "And God said, Let there be…" and each day ends with "And the evening and morning were the _____ day." Between those statements is the record of what God created on that day.

Again each day begins with "And God said…" and ends with "The evening and the morning were the _____ day." Now I ask you on what day was the formless and void earth created? What about the darkness covering the water? When was the water created? The answer to all of the above: before the first day. Verses one and two are not part of the first day. Verse one does not say, "Let there be a heaven and earth covered with water, shrouded in darkness." It assumes their existence as a prior event.

Each Creation Day Was Building on Previously Existing Material Revealed in Verses One and Two

On the **first day,** the only thing created was light to shine on a previously existing, water-covered, darkened planet.

On the **second day,** God created a firmament called heaven (not the heaven of verse one, which is the universe) that divided the waters that were already present before the first day from the waters that were above the heaven, which would be the great deep between the universe and the third heaven.

On the **third day,** God rearranged previously existing water and earth so as to separate them into seas and continents. Both already existed in verse one before the first day.

On the **fourth day,** God created the sun and moon and lights of heaven to be placed in the firmament of heaven, which heaven existed in verse one before the first day of creation.

On the **fifth day,** God populated the waters that previously existed with sea creatures, and the air in which the spirit of God moved prior to the six days he populated with birds.

On the **sixth day,** the earth that existed in a previously formless and void state was populated with animals and insects newly created. And then God formed man from the dust of the ground, which, with all its minerals, existed under the water prior to the six days.

Putting It All Together

The only new things created during the six days were our solar system, the heaven (atmosphere that surrounds our earth), vegetation, living creatures, and finally man. This was clearly a six-day re-creation of a dark planet covered with water, containing no life and no atmosphere.

However we work out the details, it is undeniable that the six days of creation occurred sometime after the original creation of the heaven and earth. Take careful note that we do not have to go outside the text to draw these conclusions. And we have not made our argument based on Hebrew. We have not referred to Lucifer or his fall or the age of the earth. The same conclusion would be drawn from any translation in any language. It is what the ancient Hebrews observed. They didn't know why it was so, only that the text clearly indicates that the original creation was found to be formless and void before the six days of re-creation. That is Gap Creation in its rudimentary form. If Young Earthers are able to dispose of all additional arguments for a gap, this biblical evidence for a gap remains unassailable.

Young Earthers' Counterpoint

Young Earth Theorists attempt to negate this argument by asserting that Genesis 1:1–2 are just preliminary statements, something like a prologue, providing us with a summary statement of the six days. In other words, verses one and two are a brief description of the entire six days. Then in verse three and following it goes back and gives us the details.

Answer:

They disregard all the rules of grammar with their assertion. Note the appearance of the connective word *And* throughout the first chapter. After verse one it is the first word in every verse with but one exception. It introduces each step forward in the sequence of events. In grammar the *And* is called a sequencing connective, as it enables the writer to develop a logical sequence of ideas—to show chronological order, as in, "and after that, this happened." We learned this part of speech in grade school. Hebrew scholars of old assert that the same is true in the Hebrew text. Simply reading the text in any language makes it obvious that verse three follows verse two in a sequence of events. Read the whole chapter right now and note the use of *And*. Without doubt all sides of the debate would agree that beginning in verse three, *And* is employed as a sequencing connective, expressing the chronology of events. How then could one suggest that the first two uses are not expressing sequence?

Genesis 1:1 In the beginning God created the heaven and the earth.

2 And *[sequence]* the earth was without form, and void; and darkness was upon the face of the deep. **And** the Spirit of God moved upon the face of the waters.

3 And God said, Let there be light: and there was light.

Verse three, "Let there be light," is a progression from verse two, "darkness upon the face of the deep." If verse one and two are summations of the entire six days, where is the light in that summary? Where are the animals? Where is man? Why give an overview that doesn't include anything accomplished in the six days? The first two verses preview nothing that occurred during the six days. And the six days record nothing that occurred in the first two verses—darkness, water, formless and void earth, and the Spirit of God moving on the face of the waters. Nor do we see the spirit of God moving on the face of the formless planet on any of the six days.

Everything God created during the six days is said to be "very good." If the first day involved the creation of a formless planet covered in darkness, how could God have declared it very good?

Furthermore it is inconceivable that God would need to go through a chaotic stage to arrive at order and beauty. That sounds more like Progressive Creation.

Everything created in the six days is a rectifying of the

unacceptable conditions found in verses one and two.

The sequencing is logical. The Spirit of God has taken interest in a lifeless, darkened planet covered with water. In the next step, God speaks for the first time: "Let there be light; and there was light." First day, first act of creation in sequence. It couldn't be more obvious. Why fight it?

Young Earthers' Counterpoint

Some Anti-Gappers, seeing the weakness in the above view, say that the first two verses are not a short overview of the six days; rather they are a statement of what God created just prior to creating light. Like a potter must acquire a formless mass of clay before he can commence shaping it, so God began his first day by creating the basic matter from which the universe would be formed, and then he continued by creating light.

Answer:

The problem with that view is that it doesn't match the record. It is creative thinking. Pun intended. The Anti-Gap crowd asserts that the preliminary work described in verses one and two must have taken place on the first day prior to creating light. Wow! I am embarrassed for the Young Earthers standing on that argument. Remember each of the six days' creation is bracketed by "And God said" at the commencement of the day, and "the evening and morning were the _____ day" at the end of the days' work.

If verses one and two are the foundational work, as a potter preparing the clay, how is it that the heavens were created before light? The heavens are light sources.

Are we to believe that on the first day God created time, space, energy, matter, all the stars, suns, moons, and planets—in short, the entire Universe—with heaven and the angels, cherubim, and seraphim, a formless and void earth, yet he failed to mention that it was part of the first day?

I can't go on with this; I feel that I am humiliating the Anti-Gap theorists. Let's go to another proof of the Gap.

CHAPTER 8

CREATED AND MADE

Extraordinary support for the Gap Fact is found in the apportioned translation of several words. The King James Bible very accurately and consistently renders these words in line with the Hebrew text. Two words that are critical to our discussion are **created** and **made.** We will make our point from the English text and respond to the critic who resorts to the Hebrew to do a snow job on the layman.

A credentialed teacher who has a working knowledge of the original languages, or anyone who can use the many Greek and Hebrew aids available, can lead the layman into the tangled web of original languages and turn him around a couple times, knowing he will not have the foggiest idea about the facts of the Hebrew, but will choose sides according to whom he thinks is the best educated and most informed.

I studied Greek in college and learned very little. I learned much more after getting out, but I would never put my

Greek knowledge up against the King James Bible, nor up against a dark, handsome fellow selling gyro sandwiches. But I have kept company with many a professor and would-be scholar spouting original languages who were about as reliable as a Jehovah's Witness with the New World translation. If you dive into the world of Greek and Hebrew lexicons, you will see that they differ from one another about as much as the denominations differ on doctrine.

Have you ever wondered why a man writes a new lexicon when he already has twenty-five in his office? It is because he seeks to correct the "errors" in the ones he has studied for forty years. He imagines his will be better, "closer to the original," etc. None of them have a final authority in any book on the face of the earth, so if you rest your doctrine on their assertions, you are placing more faith in their conclusions than they do. Over time they change their views like a new convert watching religious broadcasting. Now that I have gotten that off my stomach, let's move on and see what the English text says.

Only God Creates

First read Genesis 1–5 and note the 10 times **created** is used and the 18 times **made** and **make** are used. It would best serve the reader's understanding to do a concordance search on the two words, examining every usage throughout the Bible. **Created** is found in the Bible 53 times and **made/make** is found 2,491 times. Every time the word **create** is used in the Bible, it is God doing the creating. Neither the English word **create**, nor the Hebrew word from which it is derived, is ever used to express anything man or the Devil have done. Creation is the sole work of God alone.

The Latin Bible dating back to the time of the early church translates the Hebrew word **bara'** (create) as **ex nihilo,** meaning "out of nothing comes something." The meaning has somewhat eroded in modern usage, but the distinctive difference can readily be observed in everyday English speech and writing. We create a masterpiece, but we make a chair, unless the chair is an entirely new design that did not previously exist, and then we might say we created a new chair in order to emphasize the originality. Obviously in the absolute sense, man cannot **create** anything, except in the abstract—poetry, music, etc. Everything we make is done by rearranging or restructuring previously existing material. God **created** trees, and we **make** a house of lumber that was **made** from trees. We **make** our walls of drywall sheets **made** of gypsum. God *created* the heaven and earth, but he **made** the firmament, the sun, and moon at a later date from preexisting material.

You really need to read all 53 uses of **create** in the King James Bible, since it accurately reflects the Hebrew and Greek. For your convenience we have recorded the 10 times **create** appears in the creation account and the 18 times **make/ made** appears.

Ten Uses of *Create*

Genesis 1:1 In the beginning God **created** the heaven and the earth.

Genesis 1:21 And God **created** great whales, and every living creature that moveth, which the waters brought forth abundantly, after their kind, and every winged fowl after his kind: and God saw that it was good.

Genesis 1:27 So God **created** man in his own image, in the image of God **created** he him; male and female **created** he them.

Genesis 2:3 And God blessed the seventh day, and sanctified it: because that in it he had rested from all his work which God **created** and made.
4 These are the generations of the heavens and of the earth when they were **created,** in the day that the LORD God made the earth and the heavens,

Genesis 5:1 This is the book of the generations of Adam. In the day that God **created** man, in the likeness of God made he him;
2 Male and female **created** he them; and blessed them, and called their name Adam, in the day when they were **created**.

After the initial creation of heaven (singular—the second of the three heavens, the universe) and earth, the only thing God created from nothing was Adam and Eve and all the living creatures. During the six days, everything else was **made** by God from previously existing material, or was a product of rearrangement, as in the case of the waters and dry land simply being separated.

The Eighteen Uses of *Made/Make* in the Creation Account

Genesis 1:7 And God **made** the firmament, and divided the waters which were under the firmament from the waters which were above the firmament: and it was so.

Genesis 1:16 And God **made** two great lights; the greater light to rule the day, and the lesser light to rule the night: he **made** the stars also *[in retrospect]*. **17** And God set them in the firmament of the heaven *[which already existed]* to give light upon the earth,

The fact that he "set them *[sun and moon]* in the firmament of the heaven" is as it would be if the solar system already existed and had a place reserved for a sun and moon, but we don't really know.

Genesis 1:25 And God **made** the beast of the earth after his kind, and cattle after their kind, and every thing that creepeth upon the earth after his kind: and God saw that it was good. **26** And God said, Let us **make** man in our image…

Both man and animals were said to be *created* and *made*, for good reason. God "**formed** man of the dust of the ground" (Genesis 2:7), which is **making** from previously existing material, but the soul and spirit of Adam was an entirely new creation. Likewise "out of the ground the LORD God **formed every beast** of the field, and every fowl of the air…" (Genesis 2:19). The bodies of living creatures were formed much as a man takes clay and forms an image, but their living spirits were created afresh. Animals do have living spirits (Ecclesiastes 3:21). The Bible is a wonderfully amazing product of divine inspiration. I stand in awe!

Genesis 1:31 And God saw every thing that he had **made**, and, behold, it was very good.

God surveys his entire six days and declares it to be very good.

Genesis 2:2 And on the seventh day God ended
his work which he had **made**; and he rested on the
seventh day from all his work which he had **made**.
3 And God blessed the seventh day, and sanctified
it: because that in it he had rested from all his work
which God **created and made.**

Here is the clincher. If anyone has doubts, this should settle
it. The summary passage observes that the work of God
involved both creating and making—two different things
as distinguished by the **and**. If creating and making are the
same thing, then verse three is nonsense.

Genesis 2:4 These are the generations of the
heavens and of the earth when they were **created**, in
the day that the LORD God **made** the **earth and
the heavens,**

There are two words in this passage that need defining to
fully appreciate the verse—**generations** and **heavens.** We
will come to that directly, but for our purposes now, we will
deal only with the words *created* and *made*.

As would be expected, both **created** and **made** are used in
reference to the creation of the heavens and earth. First, the
heavens and earth were **created,** followed by a "day" when
they were **made.**

Genesis 2:9 And out of the ground **made** the
LORD God to grow every tree that is pleasant to
the sight, and good for food; the tree of life also in
the midst of the garden, and the tree of knowledge
of good and evil.

From the ground God **made** the trees to grow. God utilized
elements present in the ground to form the trees. Like a

chemist who mixes elements in combinations that generate reactions and form new compounds, God made the trees. He didn't create them at this time because they already existed in the universe. More on this later.

Genesis 2:18 And the LORD God said, It is not good that the man should be alone; I will **make** him an help meet for him.

Eve is both created and made. Her body was a product of previously existing DNA and stem cells taken from the bone marrow of Adam's rib. God created her soul.

Genesis 2:22 And the rib, which the LORD God had taken from man, **made** he a woman, and brought her unto the man.

God **made** the woman, who was said to be "bone of my bones, and flesh of my flesh… because she was **taken out of** Man" (Genesis 2:23).

Genesis 3:1 Now the serpent was more subtil than any beast of the field which the LORD God had **made**.

Beasts were both made from the ground and created in their spirits.

Genesis 3:7 And the eyes of them both were opened, and they knew that they were naked; and they sewed fig leaves together, and **made** themselves aprons.

Adam and Eve cannot create anything but they could take vine and leaves and make a garment.

Genesis 3:21 Unto Adam also and to his wife did the LORD God **make** coats of skins, and clothed them.

God didn't create coats, he took the skins from animals and made them into coats, much as a mountain man made buckskins.

> **Genesis 5:1** This is the book of the generations of Adam. In the day that God **created** man, in the likeness of God **made** he him;

And for our final use of **created** and **made** in the creation account, we again view the clincher. God created man in one day, and made him in his own likeness. Why is the word **made** used to describe Adam's nature? God used that which previously existed to fashion Adam's nature—his own image.

I am highly impressed. I have known these facts all my knowing life. But viewing it afresh with a critical eye, I find the Bible amazing in its careful and consistent use of the words **created** and **made**. The Gap Fact stands supported like the foundations of the earth itself.

There Are Several Other Verses beyond the Creation Account That Bear on This Subject

> **Genesis 6:6** And it repented the LORD that he had **made** man on the earth, and it grieved him at his heart.
> 7 And the LORD said, I will destroy man whom I have **created** from the face of the earth; both man, and beast, and the creeping thing, and the fowls of the air; for it repenteth me that I have **made** them.

The Scripture continues to recognize the difference between created and made. God did indeed make man on the earth from the earth itself, and he created him from the breath of God.

> **Isaiah 43:7** Even every one that is called by my
> name: for I have **created** him for my glory, I have
> **formed** him; yea, I have **made** him.

This is a definitive passage. All three words are used quite appropriately. Speaking of man reflecting God's image, it is appropriate to say he was **created** for God's glory, which is a reference to his soul and spirit bearing the image of God. Then he uses the word **formed**, as in Adam was **formed** from the dust of the ground like one forms clay. His spirt was not formed; it was created. Then he enforces his use of the word **formed** by the clause "yea" which shows that what follows is an expansion of the former clause, "I have **made** him." Forming is making. Breathing the breath of life into him is creating. Isn't that the most beautiful thing you ever saw? The Bible is wonderful in its detailed accuracy!

> **Isaiah 45:12** I have **made** the earth, and **created**
> man upon it: I, even my hands, have **stretched out**
> **the heavens**, and all their host have I **commanded**.

This is another profoundly eloquent verse. God **made** the earth (not created) at the time he **created** man upon it. And contemporaneous with that he **stretched out** the heavens that were already created, and then **commanded** the previously created heavens, putting them in a new order. Made, created, stretched out, and commanded, four different verbs properly placed consistent with the Genesis account written 800 years earlier, and consistent with the Gap doctrine as well.

> **Isaiah 45:17** But Israel shall be saved in the
> LORD with an everlasting salvation: ye shall not be
> ashamed nor confounded world without end.

> **18** For thus saith the LORD that **created** the
> heavens; God himself that **formed** the earth and
> **made** it; he hath **established it**, he **created** it not
> in vain, he **formed** it to be inhabited: I am the
> LORD; and there is none else.

Here is another very explicit passage maintaining the pattern set in Genesis. God first **created** the heavens. Later he **formed** the earth that existed from the time the heavens were created. Forming was part of the making process. When he says he **established** it he is amplifying verse 17 where it says "world without end." The re-creation of the earth was the opening of a new establishment under the jurisdiction of man to be **inhabited forever**.

I feel like singing. Such beautiful Scripture makes us worship our living God and fall down in wonder at his eternal program and the exactness with which it is conveyed in Holy Scripture.

CHAPTER 9

GENERATIONS OF THE HEAVENS

Immediately following the creation account in Genesis chapter one is a five-verse summary of all events leading up to the creation of Adam and Eve.

> **Genesis 2:1** Thus the heavens and the earth were finished, and all the host of them.
> **2** And on the seventh day God ended his work which he had made; and he rested on the seventh day from all his work which he had made.
> **3** And God blessed the seventh day, and sanctified it: because that in it he had rested from all his work which God created and made.
> **4** These are the **generations** of the **heavens** and of the earth when they were **created**, in the day that the LORD God **made** the earth and the heavens,

5 And every plant of the field before it was in the earth, and every herb of the field before it grew: for the LORD God had not caused it to rain upon the earth, and there was not a man to till the ground.

There are two words in this passage that we have yet to define—*generations* and *heavens*. These two words are key to understanding the big picture. We will examine them one at a time.

Three Heavens

There are three heavens. Earth's atmosphere is the first heaven. The second heaven is what we call outer space—the universe. The third heaven is the location of God's throne—Paradise.

The Bible does not tell us when the third heaven was created, but we know it already existed when God laid the foundations of the earth (Job 38:7), and it existed when Lucifer sinned (Isaiah 14:13).

The Apostle Paul recounts an experience he had of visiting Paradise in the third heaven where God dwells.

2 Corinthians 12:2 I knew a man in Christ above fourteen years ago, (whether in the body, I cannot tell; or whether out of the body, I cannot tell: God knoweth;) such an one caught up to the **third heaven**. **4** How that he was **caught up into paradise**, and heard unspeakable words, which it is not lawful for a man to utter.

Heavens (Plural)

The following passages speak of plural heavens, revealing at least three.

Psalm 115:16 The **heaven**, even the **heavens**, are the LORD'S: but the earth hath he given to the children of men.

This passage makes a clear distinction between a single heaven and additional heavens.

Ephesians 4:10 He that descended is the same also that ascended up **far above all heavens**, that he might fill all things.)

When Jesus went back to the Father, he "**ascended up far above all heavens** [*plural*]." So the place of God's throne is above the third heaven, probably in the outer edge of it, so as to be over all.

Deuteronomy 10:14 Behold, the **heaven and the heaven of heavens** is the LORD'S thy God, the earth also, with all that therein is.

This verse is definitive. All three heavens are referenced. There is a heaven *(singular)* of heavens *(plural)*. That makes one heaven above plural heavens, which would equal at least three heavens.

1 Kings 8:27 But will God indeed dwell on the earth? behold, the **heaven and heaven of heavens** cannot contain thee; how much less this house that I have builded?

Here is another acknowledgement of the three heavens.

Psalm 148:4 Praise him, ye **heavens of heavens**, and ye waters that be above the heavens.

And yet another recognition of the three heavens. And on a side note, he mentioned the water that is above the heavens (plural); that would be above the first and second heavens, between the universe and the third heaven. But that is another subject for another day.

Now We Can Look at Our Text in Genesis 2 and Understand It

> **Genesis 1:1 In the beginning** God **created** the **heaven** *[singular]* and the earth.

In the beginning of earth's generations, God created one of the three heavens. It would be the second heaven, or universe, since it includes the earth.

There are many beginnings in the Bible, some before others. Each beginning is in reference to a particular subject. For example the book of Proverbs speaks of a beginning before the earth's beginnings: "The LORD possessed me in the beginning of his way, before his works of old. I was set up **from everlasting, from the beginning, or ever the earth was**" (Proverbs 8:22–23). Before the works of creation, God possessed wisdom. This was the beginning of all beginnings because it was "from everlasting." So the beginning in Genesis 1:1 is not the beginning of everything, just the beginning of events discussed in the chapter, the original creation of one heaven and the earth.

> **Genesis 1:8** And God called the firmament **Heaven**. And the evening and the morning were the second day.
> **9** And God said, Let the waters under the heaven be gathered together unto one place, and let the dry land appear: and it was so.

God makes (not creates) the first heaven, which is earth's atmosphere.

Genesis 2:1 Thus the **heavens** *[plural]* and the earth were finished, and all the host of them.

Thus with the creation of the first heaven within the second heaven, it can be said that the heavens (plural) and earth were finished. There is now a restored earth that is "very good" lying under the three heavens. We are not told when the third heaven was created or made.

The First Heaven

The following section describing the three heavens is adapted from my book *Eight Kingdoms*.

Birds fly in the first heaven.

Genesis 1:20 …fowl that may fly above the earth in the open firmament of heaven…

Genesis 7:23 …and the fowl of the heaven…

Revelation 19:17 …fowls that fly in the midst of heaven…

Tall structures reached into the first heaven.

Genesis 11:4 And they said, Go to, let us build us a city and a tower, whose top may reach unto heaven…

Deuteronomy 1:28 …the cities are great and walled up to **heaven**…

Rain, dew, frost, and thunder come from the first heaven.

Genesis 27:28 Therefore God give thee of the dew of heaven…

Deuteronomy 11:17 …and he shut up the **heaven**, that there be no rain…

Deuteronomy 28:12 …the **heaven** to give the rain unto thy land in his season…

1 Samuel 2:10 …out of **heaven** shall he thunder upon them…

1 Kings 18:45 …the **heaven** was black with clouds and wind…

Job 38:29 …the hoary frost of **heaven**…

Isaiah 55:10 For as the rain cometh down, and the snow from **heaven**…

The Second Heaven

Stars are in the second heaven, possibly the third as well.

Genesis 1:15 And let them be for lights in the firmament of the **heaven** to give light upon the earth: and it was so.

Genesis 22:17 …as the stars of the **heaven**…

Exodus 32:13 …I will multiply your seed as the **stars** of heaven…

The Third Heaven

God's abode is located in the third heaven.

After you get past the first heaven, it is difficult to determine where the second heaven ends and the third heaven begins. We do know that God's throne is located on a firmament supported by four cherubim. It was mobile during the vision Ezekiel saw (Ezekiel 1 and 2) and is located in or above (Ephesians 4:10) the vast third heaven. From the description in Ezekiel, we recognize the four cherubim as in the same class as the four living creatures before the throne of God mentioned in Revelation 4 and 5. The name of God's abode is not **heaven**. The term *heaven* when denoting God's abode refers more than anything else to a direction (up from the earth) than to an actual place. At the end of the Millennium, God's throne will come down out of the heavens, having been converted into the New Jerusalem, to sit on the earth as its capital city (Revelation 21:2).

1 Kings 8:30 And hearken thou to the supplication of thy servant, and of thy people Israel, when they shall pray toward this place: and hear thou in heaven thy dwelling place: and when thou hearest, forgive.

Heaven is mentioned twice in the following passage. The first time, it is clearly a reference to the first heaven, and the second time, it is the place from which God hears prayers. The Bible usually fails to differentiate between the three heavens, because from a human perspective, everything that is up and beyond is heaven.

1 Kings 8:35 When **heaven is shut up,** and there is no rain, because they have sinned against thee; if they pray toward this place, and confess thy name, and turn from their sin, when thou afflictest them: **36** Then hear thou in **heaven**, and forgive the sin of thy servants, and of thy people Israel, that thou teach them the good way wherein they should walk, and give rain upon thy land, which thou hast given to thy people for an inheritance.

Again, two heavens are spoken of in the same passage—the place where God dwells and the heaven above one's head. Both alike are heaven, in that they are the created space beyond the earth.

1 Kings 8:49 Then hear thou their prayer and their supplication in heaven thy dwelling place, and maintain their cause,

54 And it was so, that when Solomon had made an end of praying all this prayer and supplication unto the LORD, he arose from before the altar of the LORD, from kneeling on his knees with his **hands spread up to heaven**.

Note that the throne of God is not heaven itself, but is **set**—located—in heaven.

Revelation 4:2 And immediately I was in the spirit: and, behold, a throne was set in heaven, and one sat on the throne.

God is said to **walk** in the circuit of heaven with a covering of clouds, which means that the throne of his presence can move about (and did in Ezekiel's vision) in that outer star region.

Job 22:12 Is not God in the height of heaven? and behold the height of the stars, how high they are!

13 And thou sayest, How doth God know? can he judge through the dark cloud?

14 Thick clouds are a covering to him, that he seeth not; and he walketh in the **circuit of heaven**.

Note in the following verse that God sits in the heavens (plural), which must be the second and third heaven.

Psalm 2:4 He that sitteth in the heavens shall laugh: the Lord shall have them in derision.

God's **throne—his holy temple**—is located in that region called heaven—the third heaven, no doubt.

Psalm 11:4 The LORD is in his holy temple, the LORD'S throne is in heaven: his eyes behold, his eyelids try, the children of men.

Generations

This is the second of two words we need to define.

Genesis 2:4 These are the **generations** of the **heavens** and of the earth when they were created, in the day that the LORD God made the earth and the heavens,

The word *generation/generations* appears in the Bible 225 times, so it will be an easy word to define with clear specificity. Every Bible reader is familiar with it, for it appears in most books of the Old Testament, 37 times in the gospels, and many times in the epistles. That is what makes this first appearance striking—surprising even. For out of the 225 uses, 224 are clear references to ancestry. The word *generate* comes from the Latin *generāre*, meaning "to beget." A grandfather is two generations—two begettings—earlier. One's father is the former generation. The present generation is living now. Future generations are the children of the present generation, and so on.

This generation is more familiar with electronics than the older generation. The young adults are getting their fifth generation iPhones. Genesis 1:1 speaks of Earth Version E1. Starting in verse three, God releases Earth Version E2. At the end of the Millennium, God will stop his support for E2 and will issue his final E3 version of earth. By then he will have all the bugs worked out and Satan will never be able to hack it again.

When you read a good portion of the 225 uses of *generations* in the Bible, the definition becomes crystal clear. For example:

> **Matthew 1:17** So all the **generations** from Abraham to David are fourteen **generations**; and from David until the carrying away into Babylon are fourteen **generations**; and from the carrying away into Babylon unto Christ are fourteen **generations**.

> **Matthew 1:1** The book of the **generation** of Jesus Christ, the son of David, the son of Abraham.
> **2** Abraham **begat** Isaac; and Isaac **begat** Jacob; and Jacob **begat** Judas and his brethren… *[and it continues with a list of the lineage of Jesus Christ down to Joseph, his stepfather, from whom he took his Jewish identity]*

Through scanning a portion of the 225 uses of *generations*, we see clearly that it is linked to the word *beget/begat*. One is begotten by his former generation and begets his next generation. Let us review the second and third use of generations in Genesis.

> **Genesis 5:1** This is the book of the generations of Adam. In the day that God created man, in the likeness of God made he him;
> **3** And Adam lived an hundred and thirty years, and **begat a son in his own likeness, after his image**; and called his name Seth:

> **Genesis 6:9** These are the **generations** of Noah: Noah was a just man and perfect in his **generations**, and Noah walked with God.
> **10** And Noah begat three sons, Shem, Ham, and Japheth.

In both passages above, *generations* speaks of successive lineage—one begotten by the other, in order.

Having reviewed a number of the uses of *generations*, we can now apply a clear definition to the very first usage.

Generations of the Heavens

> **Genesis 2:4** These are the **generations of the heavens** and of the earth when they were created, in the day that the LORD God made the earth and the heavens,

The heavens and earth have more than one life. They have an ancestry. According to the passage, Genesis 1 is a record of generations (plural). That verse makes sense only if the heaven (singular) and earth existed before the six days beginning in Genesis 1:3. I could rest my case. It is irrefutable evidence of the Gap, given by divine inspiration, without the help of science or Hebrew lexicons. Although, let's be clear, in a contest of Hebrew interpretation, the Gapists win hands down. Early Hebrew writers reference the generations of the heavens and earth, understanding to be speaking of two different life cycles of the heavens and earth.

Is there any wonder the ancients believed in a preexisting universe? They weren't bothered by science and could just believe the text even if they didn't understand it. Would to God we had more people today who would just let the Bible rule over all scientific opinions. It would result in a great deal more scientific accuracy.

Generations and Heavens in Context

Now that we have defined all the words critical to an interpretation of the creation account, we will examine the first five verses of chapter two, which is a review of events in chapter one.

2:1 Thus the heavens and the earth were finished, and all the host of them.

Three things are said to be finished: heavens, earth, and the host of them.

Heavens

Apparently God's original blueprint called for three heavens. After the six days and the making of the first heaven, he now speaks of heavens (plural) instead of the heaven (singular), telling us that they are now finished.

Earth

The earth, having been started some time earlier, is now finished, having been furnished (made) during the six days.

All the host of them

The word *host* appears 491 times and always means "a great number or multitude."

We know there are several living creatures other than man: angels, cherubim, seraphim, beasts, living creatures, and lamps, which are the seven spirits of God. So the six days finished up creation. The earth has a new king and queen in Adam and Eve, and the stars of heaven contain all of the other living creatures.

2:2 And on the seventh day God ended his work which he had **made**; and he rested on the seventh day from all his work which he had **made**.

The vast majority of the six days did not involve creating; it was making from preexisting material. The next verse adds clarity.

2:3 And God blessed the seventh day, and sanctified it: because that in it he had rested from all his work which God **created and made.**

He makes it clear that the six days involved both **creating** and **making**—always written in that order, created first, followed by made. If the words are synonyms then the sentence construction is foolish, for by the use of the connecting word *and*, he makes a list of two—created and (also) made.

2:4 These are the **generations** of the heavens and of the earth when they were **created**, in the day that the LORD God **made** the earth and the heavens,

It seems God labors the point so no one would ever fall to the temptation of being an Anti-Gapper.

Looking at the sentence word by word allows it to yield up its truths:

These—plural. He is speaking of two generations.

...are—present tense. He is NOT speaking of future generations. He speaks of two generations of the heavens and earth that had occurred to that point.

...the generations—plural, more than one begetting of the heavens and earth at that point in the discussion, which was the end of the six days.

...of the heavens and earth—the text has clearly switched from heaven (singular) to heavens (plural) after the making of earth's heaven—the atmosphere.

...when they were created, in the day that the LORD God made the earth and the heavens—two generations, the first was the creation of heaven (singular) and earth; the second generation was the **making** of the earth and **heavens** (plural). Beautifully written for accuracy, and easy to understand.

...made the earth and heavens—the phrase "heaven and earth," in that order, is found in the Bible 31 times. Additionally, "heavens and **the** earth" is found 12 times, and many more times heaven and earth are referenced together. The order speaks to the chronology of events. But only this once is earth mentioned before heavens. Why? With the introduction of light upon the dark planet, and the announcement that it was the first day, the earth was **made** anew. On the second day, God made the heaven of this earth—the atmosphere. So in the sequence of events the earth was made before the heaven. Wow again! How marvelous are thy words, O God!

...in the day that the LORD God made the earth and the heavens, [5] And every plant of the field before it was in the earth, and every herb of the field before it grew... This is an Anti-Gap killer. "God made...every plant of the field **before it was in the earth, and every herb before it grew.**" If they were made before they were in the earth, where were they cultivated? A family plants trees and herbs and then decides to relocate, so they dig up their prized plants and transfer them to their new home. If you think earth is all there is to God's creation, you are in for a very pleasant surprise. God loves plants and animals, having both in paradise.

Heirloom Seeds

What's that? What did you say? How do I know that trees and animals already existed? Have you not noted that there are trees and corn crops in heaven? Revelation 2:7 tells us that there are **trees "in the midst of the paradise of God."** As to corn previously existing, when an emergency situation arose in the wilderness with about three million people starving to death, God established a food relief ministry by opening the doors of heaven and raining down the corn of heaven, which was said to be angels' food. It was corn grown in heaven for angels to eat. Read it yourself:

> **Psalm 78:23** Though he had commanded the clouds from above, and **opened the doors of heaven**,
> **24** And had rained down manna upon them to eat, and had given them of the **corn of heaven**.
> **25** Man did eat **angels' food**: he sent them meat to the full.

Even God likes to take walks in a garden in the evening (Genesis 3:8), so, using previously existing plants, "**the LORD God planted a garden eastward in Eden**" (Genesis 2:8). When we want to plant a garden, we go to a nursery and purchase plants. God imported plants most appropriate for the garden in which he would place the newly created couple, whom he instructed to "dress it and to keep it" (Genesis 2:15). So we can say God created only one vocation—gardening. We also call it farming.

On a side note, did you notice that God is not a no-till farmer? Read 2:5 again—"no man to **till** the ground."

And another side note: When God finished the creation of the green belt, he evaluated the results "and God saw that it was good" (Genesis 1:21). Scientists have disagreed with God and have genetically modified the foods we eat. Now that they have changed what God said was good, are the plants still good? Food for thought.

He Rides a White Horse

And there are animals in Paradise (heaven)—birds too! How do I know? The B-I-B-L-E. Can you imagine that God would spend a lonely eternity without lovely flamingos and parrots and fields full of horses when he could do other-wise? God has a large ranch absolutely full of white horses (Revelation 19:11–14). Elijah was accompanied to heaven by a chariot pulled by horses (2 Kings 2:11). God has been known to receive prayer requests from between the horns of the unicorns (Psalm 22:21). Have you ever seen a unicorn? Of course not. It is an animal found only in paradise—one of God's favorites. And the throne (third heaven) is surrounded by four beasts sporting the faces of an ox, a lion, a man, and an eagle. I suppose you want to know if your dog is going to go to heaven. I don't know that one. The Bible is silent except for one very unfavorable verse (Revelation 22:15).

Let's take one more pass. The passage says the plants were made before they were in the earth. If the plants preexisted this making-of-the-earth event, then they preexisted the six days. If the plants preexisted the six days, then the six days were not the beginning of creation. The heaven and earth had already gone through one generation before the six days. Acknowledge it, dear Watson. It's elementary. Enough of having fun; time to move on.

CHAPTER 10

ANSWERS**NO**TINGENESIS.ORG

The website <u>answersingenesis.org</u> publishes chapter 5 of Ken Ham's *The New Answers Book 1*.

He starts with the same misinformation used by all the other Anti-Gap theorists. They just parrot each other without actually investigating.

> "Because of the accepted teachings of evolution, many Christians have tried to place a gap of indeterminate time between the first two verses of Genesis 1." [1]

> "Most ruin-reconstruction theorists have allowed the fallible theories of secular scientists to determine the meaning of Scripture and have, therefore, accepted the millions-of-years dates for the fossil record." [1]

---

1   Ham's arguments (1–7) and other quotations attributed to him in this chapter are all taken from: https://answersingenesis.org/ genesis/gap-theory/what-about-the-gap-and-ruin-reconstruction-theories/

Having reviewed the actual facts, you know he is misleading the reader as to the origin of the Gap Doctrine. If what he said is true, then we need to look no further—Gap proponents are stupid, liberal apostates who trust science instead of the Bible. Of course, that is the impact he wants to make with his straw-man falsehood.

Problems with the "Gap Theory" according to Ham

Ham has a section titled "Problems with the Gap Theory,"[1] where he lists seven supposed problems with the Gap Doctrine.

Ham's First Argument

> "It is inconsistent with God creating *everything* in six days, as Scripture states. Exodus 20:11 says, 'For in six days the Lord made the heavens and earth, the sea, and all that is in them, and rested the seventh day. Therefore the Lord blessed the Sabbath day, and hallowed it.'"[1]

Answer

We have already reviewed this concept twice, but because of its importance to the discussion, we will hit it one more time. He claims the passage says God created everything, including the heavens and earth in six days. But the passage does not say he **created** everything; it says he **made** the heavens and **made** the earth. And whereas Genesis 1:1 says he created **heaven** (singular) and earth, this passage says he made the **heavens** (plural) and earth. Why the change from singular to plural? Because originally, in Genesis 1:1, God created a single heaven and earth. But during the six days he **made**, not created, another heaven—the atmosphere around the earth—and he remade the earth. This passage he references speaks of the six days of making, not the first act of creating; the terminology is as we would expect in a Gap Creation scenario. It is his failure to allow two different words, **created** and **made**, to be two different words with two different meanings. He tries to make synonyms out of them, which we have proven is preposterous. Originally God created a single heaven and earth; later in an act of restoration he **made** the heavens (plural) and earth from the material of the first creation.

Ham's Third Argument

(I am going to answer his second argument last because of its length.)

> "The gap theory is logically inconsistent because it explains away what it is supposed to accommodate—supposed evidence for an old earth. Gap theorists accept that the earth is very old—a belief based on geologic evidence interpreted with the assumption that the present is the key to the past." [1]

Answer

Ham takes the liberty to tell us what motivates us to hold to Gap Creationism—accommodating geological evidence for an old earth. I have already proven by the antiquity of the Gap Doctrine that it arose from Bible exegesis alone, long before there was any geology. He sees everything through the lens of science and how one responds to it, thinking we feel threatened and are accommodating. We don't have that much respect for the opinions of secularized geologists to form our views on their vacillating pronouncements.

He then says we "accept that the earth is very old." [1] The fact is we are passive regarding any conclusion of science as to the age of the earth and universe. We know they differ. We know they will change. We know they are biased and probably wrong. But we don't care. We just want to tell them about our amazing Creator God who has a wonderful plan for the human race, and "Through faith we understand that the worlds were framed by the word of God, so that things which are seen were not made of things which do appear" (Hebrews 11:3). We don't wear Ham's colored glasses. He is trying to draw us into a revolution we don't want to fight because we are too busy trying to evangelize.

Ham's Fourth Argument

"The gap theory does away with the evidence for the historical event of the global Flood.

If the fossil record was formed by Lucifer's flood, then what did the global Flood of Noah's day do? On this point the gap theorist is forced to conclude that the global Flood must have left virtually no trace. To be consistent, the gap theorist would also have to defend that the global Flood was a local event." [1]

Answer

This is strange reasoning. He assumes that we Bible believers are concerned with geology, that we are navigating our doctrine according to prevailing secular opinions. He has us confused with his own kind. There is a great host of us out here who come from a long line of just believing the Scripture. We are not in your cage match, so don't try to drag us in.

And he tells us that we Gap proponents **"would also have to defend that the global Flood was a local event."** [1] You see, we never claimed that all fossil record is a result of Lucifer's flood. We don't know or care. My uneducated guess would be that some of it was, and the greater part of it is a result of Noah's flood and the division of the earth that followed the flood (1 Chronicles 1:19). But it could be that the earth was so thoroughly destroyed in its formless and void state that it was left void of any evidence of the former inhabitants, and that all geological records are a product of a young earth and God's efforts to make it look old. We don't care if Young Earthers prove it is six thousand years old or secularists prove it is six billion years old. That is a battle that has nothing to do with the Creation Gap.

Ham's Fifth Argument

"The gap theorist ignores the evidence for a young earth.

The true gap theorist also ignores evidence consistent with an earth fewer than 10,000 years of age. There is much evidence for this—the decay and rapid reversals of the earth's magnetic field, the amount of salt in the oceans, the wind-up of spiral galaxies, and much more." [1]

Answer

We are not only ignoring the evidence for a young earth, we are ignoring evidence for an old earth. And we were ignoring you until you got in the way of our evangelism and drew away a segment of the church to place more faith in Scientism than in Holy Scripture.

We are glad for you to display your evidence for a young earth and to debate with old earth geologists. It is fun to watch. But it has nothing to do with the church or the Word of God. The earth as we can know it may be less than 10,000 years old. We have never had a problem with a young earth.

But it concerns us that you borrow the authority of Holy Scripture to bolster your scientific opinions, and, in the process, denigrate traditional Bible doctrine that has been around ever since the apostles.

Ham's Sixth Argument

"The gap theory fails to accommodate standard uniformitarian geology with its long ages.

Today's uniformitarian geologists allow for no worldwide flood of any kind—the imaginary Lucifer's flood or the historical Flood of Noah's day. They also recognize no break between the supposed former created world and the current recreated world." [1]

Answer

Ham is still seeing everything though the eyes of science. That is why we call his position Scientism, because it exalts science above all things.

It is almost funny. He charges us with accommodating geology and then says one of the problems with the Gap is that it "fails to accommodate standard uniformitarian geology," [1] as if that were our goal all along. This is bizarre. He is arguing with himself.

Ham's Second Argument

He has two arguments left, the second and the seventh. I saved them for last because they require a longer answer.

"It puts death, disease, and suffering before the Fall, contrary to Scripture.

Romans 5:12 says, "Therefore, just as through one

man *[Adam]* sin entered the world, and death through sin, and thus death spread to all men, because all sinned." From this we understand that there could not have been human sin or death before Adam. The Bible teaches in 1 Corinthians 15 that Adam was the first man, and as a result of his rebellion (sin), death and corruption (disease, bloodshed, and suffering) entered the universe. Before Adam sinned, there could not have been any animal (nephesh) or human death. Note also that there could not have been a race of men before Adam that died in Lucifer's flood because 1 Corinthians 15:45 tells us that Adam was the first man." [1]

Answer

We will deal with the misinformation first. To start with, he uses a corrupted, commercial translation that is in grave error. Among other inaccuracies in the text, it says, "death **spread to** all men." The Holy Bible says "death **passed upon** all men." One translation is correct; the other isn't, for they are in conflict. Did death "**spread**" as if it were a contagion contracted one person at a time in an ever widening circle? That is heresy. Death "**passed upon**" all men in the one act of Adam. It did not spread through contact. Where did he get such a silly translation?

The passage is drawing a parallel between the work of Adam and the work of Christ. Both acted on behalf of their posterity, their actions being counted as the actions of all who were in them. One man sinned and all died. One man obeyed, died for sin, and was raised, so all men in Christ obeyed, died, and were raised. In the non-translation Ham uses, if Adam's sin resulted in sin spreading to the human race, then Christ's actions resulted in atonement spreading to the human race. I know that no God-respecting Calvinist would fancy that wording. So if Ham is going to try to stand on Scripture, he should first acquire a copy.

I know this is not relevant to our subject, but I couldn't let that kind of heresy pass while he is charging us with doing dishonor to the passage.

Read the passage in the KJV.

> **Romans 5:12** Wherefore, as by one man sin entered into the **world**, and death by sin; and so death **passed upon** all men, for that all have sinned:

Now read it in the corrupted version that is Ham's favorite.

> **"Romans 5:12** Therefore, just as through one man [Adam] sin entered the **world**, and death through sin, and thus death **spread** to all men, because all sinned." [1]

Either version will make our point. Look at the passage objectively. What does it say? It says that though the act of one man sin entered into the world and brought death upon the human race. **The place where the sin occurred is the world, not the universe**. It does not say that sin did not exist outside the world. It doesn't say that Lucifer had not previously sinned in heaven when he lied, murdered, and attempted to displace God on the throne. Ham stretches our sense of the rational with his "interpretation" of the passage.

Ham says, **"The Bible teaches in 1 Corinthians 15 that Adam was the first man, and as a result of his rebellion (sin), death and corruption (disease, bloodshed, and suffering) <u>entered the universe</u>."** [1] Oh, oh, oh, no; there you go again. Death entered the **universe**? If it says "universe" then I should withdraw my book from the market, for it would be wrong. If Adam committed the first sin **in the**

universe, then Lucifer did not sin before Adam and Eve. And Eve did not sin before Adam. If, as Ham asserts, the Bible says Adam committed the first sin in the universe, then your Bible is pretty much worthless, for it lacks cohesion and is self-contradictory. It would be about as jumbled and mixed up as the Quran in its chronology of the Old Testament patriarchs.

The word **universe** never appears anywhere in the Bible. And no translation in any language, not even the most corrupt, says Adam committed the first sin in the universe. The Bible says "**world**." That is much smaller than the universe.

Ham says, "**Note also that there could not have been a race of men before Adam that died in Lucifer's flood because 1 Corinthians 15:45 tells us that Adam was the first man.**" [1] Where did that come from? Who asserts that there was a race of men before Adam? It was angels, who were called gods (Psalm 82:6), not men, that Lucifer led into rebellion.

The bottom line is that the passage speaks of the human race alone, located on this planet, freshly renovated and re-created so as to be "very good," with no sin or death in it until Lucifer came from without and introduced it to Eve.

Who Was the First Sinner?

Furthermore, if you take Lucifer and all the fallen angels out of the equation; if they had not sinned or died before Adam, then with certainty we could still say that Adam was not the first sinner on the earth, for Eve sinned before Adam did.

> **1 Timothy 2:14** And Adam was not deceived, but the woman being deceived **was in the transgression.**

Since Eve sinned before Adam, how is it that sin did not enter the world until Adam sinned? Because Adam was the head of the human race (the federal head), and until he sinned and corrupted his seed, sin and death could not pass upon all men.

Now follow carefully. This is the clincher. Since the Scripture has ignored Eve's sin—it not causing sin to enter the world—that tells us that **Romans 5:12 is not a statement about the first sin in the universe**, **nor the first sin in the world**; it is about the first man sinning. When Eve sinned before Adam, it did not affect Adam's posterity, and sin did not enter the world through Eve. Likewise when Lucifer and the angels sinned, sin did not enter the world, and all humans did not become sinners. However, when the representative head of the human race sinned, it introduced sin and death into the human race (the world), not because it was the first sin ever committed, but because it was the first sin committed by the head of the human race. Elementary, my dear Watson.

Again, Ham quotes a corrupted version of Romans 5:12 and asserts, "**From this we understand that there could not have been human sin or death before Adam.**" [1] But there was sin before Adam—Eve. And we know from the vast amount of Scripture that Lucifer and the angels sinned before Adam, but not being members of the human race, their sin had no bearing on Adam's posterity. This is too easy.

Ham's Seventh and Final Argument

"Most importantly, the gap theory undermines the gospel at its foundations.

By accepting an ancient age for the earth (based on the standard uniformitarian interpretation of the

geologic column), gap theorists leave the evolutionary system intact (which by their own assumptions
they oppose)." [1]

Answer

I am compelled to interrupt his flow with a comment. He
says **we accept "an ancient age for the earth (based on the
standard uniformitarian interpretation of the geologic
column)."** [1] Liar, liar, pants on fire. We do not. He is in the
wrong classroom.

Ham Continues

"Even worse, they must also theorize that Romans
5:12 and Genesis 3:3 refer only to spiritual death. But this contradicts other scriptures,
such as 1 Corinthians 15 and Genesis 3:22–
23. These passages tell us that Adam's sin led
to physical death, as well as spiritual death. In
1 Corinthians 15 the death of the Last Adam
(the Lord Jesus Christ) is compared with the death
of the first Adam. Jesus suffered physical death for
man's sin, because Adam, the first man, died physi-
cally because of sin.

To believe there was death before Adam's sin destroys
the basis of the Christian message. The Bible states
that man's rebellious actions led to death and the
corruption of the universe, but the gap theory undermines the reason that man needs a Savior." [1]

Answer

He starts off by saying, **"they must also theorize that
Romans 5:12 and Genesis 3:3 refer only to spiritual**

death."[1] And then he answers the argument he attributed to our position. That my dear friends (and enemies) is a prime example of building a straw-man argument—one he could safely tear down without incurring battle fatigue. I don't know of anyone who believes what he imagined. Furthermore I don't believe there is any such thing as spiritual death. Type it into your search engine and look up every time the word spirit or spiritual appears in the Bible. Search for the word death appearing with spiritual. You will be shocked. **There is no such thing as a man with a dead spirit.** The Bible acknowledges the presence of a human spirit in fallen and reprobate men.

There is only one death that passed upon the human race, and it is physical.

> **1 Corinthians 15:21** For since by man came death, by man came also the resurrection of the dead.
> **22** For as in Adam all die, even so in Christ shall all be made alive.
> **23** But every man in his own order: Christ the firstfruits; afterward they that are Christ's at his coming.

The death incurred is cured by the resurrection of the human body, not by regeneration. The death incurred in Adam is not rectified until the coming of Jesus Christ. If there were a spiritual death, it would be cured at the new birth. But Adam's death is cured only with a resurrected body.

So don't accuse this Gap Creationist of not believing Adam incurred physical death upon the human race when he sinned.

We do not do disservice to the atonement of Christ by believing that sin and death existed in the universe before our federal head took us with him into sin and death. You do disservice to God's redeemed. Just leave us out of the science debate. And stay away from our sacred text, altering the words and telling us what we believe about it. We will continue to believe what our forefathers have believed for over 2,000 years.

Ham Says

> "To believe there was death before Adam's sin destroys the basis of the Christian message." [1]

This is a manufactured argument that has no basis in reality. Our "Christian message" is still bringing redemption to the most hardened criminals in the worst prisons, to dopeheads and homosexuals, and to our children and grandchildren, just like it did to my grandmother, father, mother, and brothers and sisters. Suppositions and imaginations concocting irrational arguments that do not address the issue will never convince thinking men and women who believe their King James Bible.

Another "Problem"

> Ham says: "The version of the gap theory that puts Satan's fall at the end of the geological ages, just before the supposed Lucifer's flood that destroyed all pre-Adamic life, has a further problem—the death and suffering recorded in the fossils must have been God's fault. Since it happened before Satan's fall, Satan and sin cannot be blamed for it." [1]

Answer

He makes two unsupported assumptions.

First assumption: He assumes that Satan's fall resulted in immediate judgment on the earth. Look at the pattern;

always look at the pattern. God will eventually destroy this earth and make a new one. Did God destroy the earth immediately after Adam sinned? I think not. Did God immediately send the Flood on the world when he declared them worthy of death? Then why so confident that God would have immediately judged the world after Lucifer's sin? Lucifer is the first liar and murderer (John 8:44). Did he commit those sins in his initial assault upon the throne, or did he commit them later? We don't know. When the Bible begins, those events are all in the past and are not the subject of the Bible. Only little tidbits are recorded in passing.

Second assumption: He assumes we profess that the fossil records of death and ruin are a product of the former earth under the angels. Not so. We are not geologists and don't dabble in it. How can we know the source or timing of an old bone or an oil deposit seven miles deep in the earth? If indeed we claimed that all the geological records of death and ruin are a result of Lucifer's deluge, then you would have to refer to our belief as "Gap Creation Scientism." I'm not going there.

I believe in a Gap because the Bible tells me so, not because of a series I viewed on Public Broadcasting about dinosaur bones and sea shells in Shelby, South Dakota, and not because I attended a seminar put on by a Creation Science Apostle immersed in Scientism.

The First Sinner

Finally, and this one is amazing to me. It makes the Creation Scientism position look absurd. If there was no sin or death anywhere in the universe before Adam's sin, how did a sinful, disembodied cherub get in the garden to tempt Eve at the end of the sixth day? That is a question that would shut down a Christian Scientism press conference.

CHAPTER 11

THROUGH FAITH
WE UNDERSTAND

Modern Creation Scientists have risen up to combat evolution with the very tools of science—a most worthy pursuit
by those with recognized credentials who can wield the sword
of science on the academic battlefield. But the scientific
debate should not be viewed as an evangelistic tool. Creation
Scientists are trying to use science to convince secularists of
Spoken Word Creation—a conclusion that can only be held
by faith. "**Through faith we understand that the worlds were
framed by the word of God, so that things which are seen
were not made of things which do appear**" (Hebrews 11:3).
Science cannot prove that God created the earth recently with
the appearance of age any more than it can prove the resurrection of Jesus Christ or the existence of heaven and hell.
Solomon observed, "no man can find out the work that God
maketh from the beginning to the end" (Ecclesiastes 3:11).

Unbelievers are not lacking in science; they are lacking in faith, and **saving faith cannot come by the proofs of science**. "So then faith cometh by hearing, and hearing by the word of God" (Romans 10:17).

Young Earth Scientism Is a Misdirection

Young Earthism is a misdirection that has hindered the gospel of Jesus Christ. It directs the natural man to focus on the arguments of science rather than the person of Jesus Christ. It directs men to look to their intellects rather than to their hearts, to empirical evidence rather than to spiritual realities.

> **1 Corinthians 2:7** But we speak the wisdom of God in a mystery, even the **hidden wisdom**, which God ordained before the world unto our glory:
> **8** Which none of the princes of this world knew: for had they known it, they would not have crucified the Lord of glory.
> **9** But as it is written, Eye hath not seen, nor ear heard, neither have entered into the heart of man, the things which God hath prepared for them that love him.
> **10** But God hath **revealed them unto us by his Spirit**: for the Spirit searcheth all things, yea, the deep things of God.
> **11** For what man knoweth the things of a man, save the spirit of man which is in him? even so **the things of God knoweth no man, but the Spirit of God.**
> **12** Now we have received, not the spirit of the world, but the spirit which is of God; **that we might know the things that are freely given to us of God.**
> **13** Which things also we speak, **not in the words which man's wisdom teacheth**, but which the

Holy Ghost teacheth; comparing spiritual things
with spiritual.

14 But the natural man receiveth not the things
of the Spirit of God: for they are foolishness unto
him: neither can he know them, **because they are
spiritually discerned.**

The above passage speaks of hidden wisdom that is not acces-
sible by natural means nor by wisdom that can be taught.
Rather, the Spirit of God makes enquiry on our behalf into
the hidden things of God and reveals them directly to our
spirit. Spirit answers to spirit in this divine communication
unknown by learned wisdom. That knocks my socks off!

Paul said to the Corinthians, "For Christ sent me not to
baptize, but to preach the gospel: **not with wisdom of
words**, lest the cross of Christ should be made of none effect"
(1 Corinthians 1:17). Apparently, it is possible to render the
gospel message ineffective if it is shrouded in wisdom of words.

Someone said there is a God-shaped hole in the heart of
every man. Creation Scientists are trying to fill that hole
with science, but the only thing that will fill it is God, and
that by faith alone, not irrefutable proofs.

John 12:32 And I, if I be lifted up from the earth,
will draw all men unto me.

Young Earthism attempts to convert the mind of those
predisposed to not believe. Rather than provide evidence,
Jesus would simply have said, "What saith the Scriptures?"
Thomas Chalkley wisely observed, "There are none so blind
as those who will not see. The most deluded people are those
who choose to ignore what they already know." (*A Collection
of Works of Thomas Chalkley*, 1713).

Faith Is the Matrix

God bypasses the scientific steps: observation, question, hypothesis, experiment, and analysis of the data. He approaches men on a different plane—Spirit to spirit. "God is a Spirit: and they that worship him must worship him in spirit and in truth" (John 4:24). "The **Spirit itself beareth witness with our spirit**, that we are the children of God:" (Romans 8:16). God says they "shew the work of the law **written in their hearts**, their conscience also bearing witness…" (Romans 2:15).

Young Earth Scientists and their disciples expect scientific evidence to lead to faith, but God imparts faith only in response to believing on Jesus Christ. While we desire evidence to validate the unseen, God desires faith in the unseen with no evidence other than the internal witness of the Spirit in response to hearing his words. **You need to read that again.**

> **Hebrews 11:1** Now faith is the substance of things hoped for, the evidence of things not seen.

The passage says, faith is **substance**, faith is **evidence,** of things **hoped for** but **not seen**. In this passage there is nothing seen that can be considered evidence for faith. Rather, in the absence of scientific evidence, the supernatural presence of faith is testimony—is evidence—of the reality of things not seen. If that seems to be contrary to the laws of logic, that is because it is a different logic—logic of the spirit. The entire eleventh chapter of Hebrews is based on the principle of believing with no evidence to support the faith other than the promise of God. **That is not blind faith; it is faith based on the substance and evidence of the spirit within**. There is a compelling force within every person to conform to the will of God. It is an innate knowledge that is inescapable except when the heart is harden by repeated rejection of that inner witness (Hebrews 3:8–11).

> **Romans 1:19** Because that which may be known of God is manifest in them; for God hath shewed it unto them.
>
> **20** For the **invisible things** of him from the creation of the world **are clearly seen**, being **understood** by the things that are made, even his eternal power and Godhead; so that they are without excuse:

Invisible things of God are clearly seen within through the witness of God's Spirit to our spirit. Every person has within him, as part of his created nature, an understanding of the Godhead. **So there are two avenues to faith. One is spiritual and the other is empirical**. The spiritual leads to a spiritual rebirth. The empirical leads to greater intellectual confidence in the facts. Both are valuable, but **only faith in the unseen restores one to fellowship with God.**

The concept of faith in the unseen being substantive and evidentiary is contrary to all physical law. But it is the heart of spiritual law. **God has designed that faith should be the matrix of all that is redemptive, restorative, creative, righteous, and of good report** (Hebrews 11). We are created to live in fellowship rooted in faith. All meaningful interpersonal relationships are built on faith. Faith takes us deeper and makes relationships more meaningful and much richer in love than is otherwise possible. For the sake of human/divine communion, **God deliberately concealed the age of the universe and its origin so as to make faith essential to understanding creation**.

Faith is indeed the vehicle to God's blessings, but, much more, **it is the sanctified state itself**. God desires people of faith. **"But without faith it is impossible to please him"** (Hebrews 11:6). Adam didn't lose faith in the evidence; he lost faith in God personally. In order to be restored to sonship, God requires only one thing—a relationship of faith (trust, dependence, openness, sharing, communing, confidence, etc.). **Faith is not just a means to the grace of God; it is the fulfilment of God's eternal purpose in man**. God's original intention was to have faith-full sons. Any shortcut that limits the full expression of faith is the enemy of God's program. Creation Scientism substitutes faith with arguable facts.

Jesus Did Not Accept Their Faith

God does not welcome faith that is prompted by the facts. **To surrender to your enemy because of his overwhelming superiority does not make you a loyal subject of the new regime**. Likewise, surrender to a belief because of overwhelming evidence does not make one a thankful recipient of grace.

> **John 2:23** Now when he was in Jerusalem at the passover, in the feast day, **many believed in his name**, when they saw the miracles which he did.
> **24** But Jesus did not commit himself unto them, because he knew all men,
> **25** And needed not that any should testify of man: for he knew what was in man.

This is an amazing passage. Jesus is surrounded with unbelief. He performs miracles, providing proof of his identity, but when **"many believed in his name"** in response to overwhelming proof, he stepped back and rejected their faith because he knew what was in their hearts. Faith springing from intellectual proofs brings the mind and will to bay but not the heart. A man convinced by undeniable proof will in his heart still stand aloof. God is not interested in creating faith from facts; **he wants to see faith develop from fellowship** with Jesus Christ.

There is no praise and honor when an enemy believes in you because you overwhelmed him with undeniable proofs. But there is great honor when a friend believes in you without evidence, or in the face of contradicting evidence, simply because he knows your heart and trusts you over all evidence to the contrary (Romans 4:17–21).

To choose Christ is to choose the truth that is in one's heart. To reject Christ for lack of external evidence is to ignore a greater witness in one's own spirit. It is silencing the cries of one's spirit for want of a different voice with a different message. Belief and unbelief manifest the condition of the heart.

Our goal as evangelists is to make Christ known to the natural man. We don't do that with reason, argument, or proofs; we do it by modeling the beauty of his love and forgiveness and speaking of his person as revealed in the biblical record of his life and teachings. If you had a friend far away that you loved and you wanted another friend close at hand to love him too, then your conversation would be that of an evangelist.

Hebrews chapter eleven provides a long list of people who believed God against circumstances that would have caused others to turn away in doubt. The entire earth and human experience is rigged by God to make faith difficult, to try our faith with reasons to doubt (1 Peter 1:7; James 1:3), so that those who believe will be near to the heart of God (Hebrews 10:22, 38).

Jesus was not careful to phrase his responses so as to prevent misunderstanding or to not cause offence. Rather he gave occasion for his disciples to not believe, testing their faith in him, as we see in John chapter six. When they wrestled with their understanding, he responded, "It is the **spirit that quickeneth**; the flesh profiteth nothing: the **words that I speak unto you, they are spirit, and they are life**" (John 6:63). In response to his difficult-to-understand words, "many of his disciples went back, and walked no more with him" (John 6:66). As the crowd thinned out, many former believers walking away, Jesus turned to his faithful twelve and challenged, "Will ye also go away?" "Then Simon Peter answered him, Lord, to whom shall we go? thou hast the words of eternal life. And **we believe and are sure** that thou art that Christ, the Son of the living God" (John 6:68–69). Jesus understood that his words were accompanied by his Spirit and were efficacious in producing life (1 Thessalonians 2:13). Jesus would never command the attention of an unbeliever with proofs and evidence. He would present himself, knowing there was a reality in the heart that could respond or not, and if that was not enough, he dismissed them and moved on.

I realize that in this hour of progressive Christianity this is a lost concept, but it is a biblical reality, the understanding of which must be recovered if the Christian religion is going to be any different than any other man-made religion.

Christians are not the only ones who live in a spiritual plane. Those who believe in naturalistic evolution like to think they are motivated by deductive reasoning. But there is always an emotional and spiritual component that reveals a heart disposed to advance any alternative to Spoken Word Creation because of its implications regarding responsibility and accountability toward a holy God. They are predisposed to unbelief. Their resistance, though couched in intellectual terms, is actually a heart issue that can be healed only with repentance toward God, not repentance toward the facts. I think we forget that the evolutionist walks after "the spirit that now worketh in the children of disobedience" (Ephesians 2:2). So we should address them as did the Apostle Paul:

> **1 Corinthians 2:4** And my speech and my preaching was **not with enticing words** of man's wisdom, but in demonstration of the Spirit and of power: **5** That your faith should not stand in the wisdom of men, but in the power of God.

> **1 Corinthians 2:2** For I determined not to know any thing among you, save Jesus Christ, and him crucified.

> **1 Corinthians 1:17** For Christ sent me not to baptize, but to preach the gospel: not with wisdom of words, lest the cross of Christ should be made of none effect.

CHAPTER 12

SINCERELY WRONG

Of no doubt, Young Earth Creationists have dedicated their resources and energies to convert evolutionists to creationism. I fully appreciate their desire to utilize science to cause natural men to acknowledge our great Creator. Their motive is good, and in a few instances the evidence they provide will be the tipping point for a person riding the fence to fully embrace creationism in opposition to evolution. And no doubt their scientific approach will at times remove intellectual resistance to hearing the gospel. I have enjoyed the fruit of a good evidentiary argument. But too often the end result of their method is to impart a public perception that has become in practice a false gospel. **Creation Gospel is false in the same vein as a Sobriety Gospel** propagated by evangelists who seek to get people off drugs and alcohol so they can become Christians. These conversion-evangelists are guilty of imparting a false impression of the gospel. Sobriety treatments are good, as is pure Scientific Creationism, when kept in perspective, but neither will produce saving faith.

I have led homosexuals to faith in Christ, but I never attempted to get them to first transition into a heterosexual lifestyle. The gospel came to them in their sinfulness and brought the new birth, which produced new life, and new life brought a new perspective on everything. They always stopped their homosexuality and eventually married the opposite sex and established a Christian family. Evangelism is from the heart out, not the head down.

If you go to sinners and make their greatest addiction the issue of repentance, you will drive them away because you have not led them to believe on Jesus Christ; you have challenged them to give up the thing most dear in their lives, and they do not have the will to do that; and most of all, they do not have a reason other than to please a religious movement, which in most cases they deem to be judgmental, less than honest, and lacking compassion. And in regard to the age of the universe, they view Christians as backward and anti-scientific. Only the presence of the Spirit of God in their hearts and a vision of Christ will motivate sinners to change their views about sin, self, and God, resulting in a change of actions.

Gospel evangelists are forced to confront the public who deem Creation Scientists and their disciples as equal to the flat-earth crowd. What these college students see as anti-science has rendered the Bible unfathomable. I will win ten biology students to faith in Christ with the Gap fact, sin fact, and Jesus fact while the Creation Scientist is debating an ignorant biology professor with nothing to show for it but another video of their debate destined to be viewed by the choir.

Schism of the Hour
Combating evolution never became a centerpiece in our evangelism, just a tool we occasionally used to wipe away

resistance to the Bible and get down to the real subject of Jesus Christ. I am afraid that today some Christians are worshiping at the altar of Young Earthism and have lost the original purpose of answering the evolutionists, which is to remove obstacles to the gospel of Christ. They don't seem to care that their insistence upon a young earth has made it harder to break down the resistance of modern secularists to the Bible. Down through the history of the church, more harm has been done to evangelism through fervent and fanatical crusades of passing fancies and folly than from outright heresy. **Young Earthism is the schism of the hour—Bible doctrine falsely so called.**

A Manufactured Argument

Why castigate the Bible and depart from traditional interpretations to establish a theory that to the average student of geology appears to be scientifically absurd?

Some may believe the geological record points to a very old earth, and others may think the record points to a very young earth. Neither derived their conclusions from the Bible. Ask a Young Earth, Anti-Gap advocate to show you a passage in the Bible that says the earth is only six thousand years old. Where is the commandment to believe such? When was the age of the earth an issue anywhere in the Bible? Do I hear stuttering?

The age of the earth, regardless of what it is, is a matter of debate for scientists, not an argument that can be supported from the Bible one way or the other. A young earth is not essential to belief in Spoken Word Creation, and certainly not essential to believing the gospel of Jesus Christ. Furthermore, the age of the earth has nothing to do with evolution. One can admit to a very old earth and still combat evolution. Young Earthism is a manufactured argument that should never be part of the creation/evolution debate. **A creation established with the appearance of age has rendered dating impossible.** A creation destroyed and then re-created only serves to put dating further out of reach.

If the earth and universe are not old, then God wasted a lot of effort making it appear so by creating it with the appearance of age. Astronomers are viewing stars up to nine billion light years away. Why blame the secular geologists for accepting the God-imparted appearance of age? The argument for or against evolution is not about the age of the earth, it is about the irreducible complexity of nature.

An Appeal

We insist that Young Earthers stop hanging the integrity of the Scriptures on their narrow scientific views. It is embarrassing, and **we keep having to explain that Young Earthism is a new Christian cult** that does not represent the historical biblical position. It has gotten to the point that when we approach a person with the message of Christ, our conversation is stalled as we try to convince them that the Bible does not teach the earth is flat, or that the earth is just six thousand years old, or that earthquakes are a sign of the end of the world, or that blood moons are an indicator that the end is near, or that Christ is coming back September 13 due to some mathematical computations and the dire meaning of the number 13. Young Earthism and Flat Earthism will fall flat and become buried in the stratification of stupid ideas, even if the earth is young, but in the meantime, it is hurting our Christian witness. So I say to Young Earth insisters, **leave us and our Bible out of your science.** It is not helping our evangelism.

If you want to appeal to science to combat evolution, stick to the issue and stop trying to prove the unprovable nonessential that is actually a matter of faith.

Testimony of a Student

"I am a chemical engineering student and I have talked to many non-believing science students, and once you truly engage them you realize that 90% of the time evolution/creation is never the real reason they give for their unbelief. Most of the time it's because they see Christianity as a religion of rules, void of grace. The only thing they ever hear about Christianity is creation/evolution people yelling about evolution. That is a far cry from preaching what has been received (1 Corinthians 15)."

The Lure of Intellectualism

I understand that it is personal with scientists who have suffered ridicule in their fields. They fight for acceptance of their professional views. To hear the secularists cry uncle is the sweetest vindication. But Young Earth zealots are not evangelists and they have often proven their inability to accurately handle the words of God, so the movement has become a nuisance and a stumbling block to traditional evangelism. They should stop it and go back to preaching the wonders and complexities of creation as Moody Institute of Science did in the fifties and sixties.

The well-informed Young Earthers who are highly invested in their arguments and have confronted many evolutionists with their scientific argument with the intention of converting them are not going to accept my charge that they hinder evangelism, for they have had many experiences where they have wowed the novice with their greater understanding and have elicited immediate surrender to their superior knowledge. Though I am not that well informed, I, too, have silenced rookie evolutionists and atheists many times, and I must admit it is fun, but it is not the gospel and does not win people to Christ. Granted, when one follows through with the gospel, as I have done, we see true conversions among science-worshiping secularists. The danger is trusting in scientific arguments, or spending too much time on them, and neglecting the cross of Christ. If one is not an extreme master of all the scientific facts, it is far better to remain silent on the subject and just share one's personal testimony of Christ.

> **1 Corinthians 2:1** And I, brethren, when I came to you, came not with excellency of speech or of wisdom, declaring unto you the testimony of God.
> **2** For I determined not to know any thing among you, save Jesus Christ, and him crucified.
> **3** And I was with you in weakness, and in fear, and in much trembling.
> **4** And my speech and my preaching was **not with enticing words of man's wisdom**, but in demonstration of the Spirit and of power:

I am afraid that we live in a day and age when the power of preaching Christ is little known and not at all cool. Whereas spouting science is self-elevating and avoids the "offence of the cross" (Galatians 5:11).

> **1 Corinthians 1:17** For Christ sent me not to baptize, but to preach the gospel: not with wisdom of words, lest the cross of Christ should be made of none effect.
> **18** For the preaching of the cross is to them that

perish foolishness; but unto us which are saved it is the power of God.

19 For it is written, I will **destroy the wisdom of the wise**, and will bring to nothing the understanding of the prudent.

20 Where is the wise? where is the scribe? where is the disputer of this world? hath not God made foolish the wisdom of this world?

21 For after that in the wisdom of God **the world by wisdom knew not God**, it pleased God by the foolishness of preaching to save them that believe.

22 For the Jews require a sign, and the Greeks seek after wisdom:

23 But we preach Christ crucified, unto the Jews a stumblingblock, and unto the Greeks foolishness;

24 But unto them which are called, both Jews and Greeks, Christ the power of God, and the wisdom of God.

25 Because the foolishness of God is wiser than men; and the weakness of God is stronger than men.

26 For ye see your calling, brethren, how that not many wise men after the flesh, not many mighty, not many noble, are called:

27 But God hath chosen the foolish things of the world to confound the wise; and God hath chosen the weak things of the world to confound the things which are mighty;

28 And base things of the world, and things which are despised, hath God chosen, yea, and things which are not, to bring to nought things that are:

29 That no flesh should glory in his presence.

I am not suggesting we should be ignorant of the facts of science. To the contrary; we should be the best informed of all men. But knowledge of science, philosophy, and other religions should be worn like a concealed weapon, not to be drawn until one is backed into a corner and there is no way out. Then we use minimal intellectual force to disarm our adversary, and in most cases just brandishing loaded knowledge is enough to de-escalate the evangelistic situation. When a Young Earther is filled with the pride of his knowledge and approaches his evangelism like a self-defense expert trolling the seedy district just hoping someone jumps him so he can put them down, he has departed from the Spirit of God and is walking after his intellectual flesh.

Fourth-Century Pseudo-Scientific Assertions

Augustine, in the fourth century, obviously had to deal with the same issue of Christians trying to dabble in the sciences, with the same ill effects as some Young Earth Creationists are producing today.

Augustine writes:

"Usually, even a non-Christian knows something about the earth, the heavens, and the other elements of this world, about the motion and orbit of the stars and even their size and relative positions, about the predictable eclipses of the sun and moon, the cycles of the years and the seasons, about the kinds of animals, shrubs, stones, and so forth, and this knowledge he holds to as being certain from reason and experience. Now, it is a disgraceful and dangerous thing for an infidel to hear a Christian, presumably giving the meaning of Holy Scripture, talking nonsense on these topics; and we should take all means to prevent such an embarrassing situation, in which people show up vast ignorance in a Christian and laugh it to scorn. The shame is not so much that an ignorant individual is derided, but that people outside the household of faith think our sacred writers held such opinions, and, to the great loss of those for whose salvation we toil, the writers of our Scripture are criticized and rejected as unlearned men. If they find a Christian mistaken in a field which they themselves know well and hear him maintaining his foolish opinions about our books, how are they going to believe those books in matters concerning the resurrection of the dead, the hope of eternal life, and the kingdom of heaven, when they think their pages are full of falsehoods and on facts which they themselves have learnt from experience and the light of reason? Reckless and incompetent expounders of Holy Scripture bring untold trouble and sorrow on their wiser brethren when they are caught in one of their mischievous false opinions and are taken to task by those who are not bound by the authority of our sacred books. For then, to defend their utterly foolish and obviously untrue statements, they will try to call upon Holy Scripture for proof and even recite from memory many passages which they think support their position, although they understand neither what they say nor the things about which they make assertion." (Augustine, *De Genesi ad litteram:* 1.19.39 translated by J.H. Taylor, Ancient Christian Writers, Newman Press, 1982, volume 41.)

That is amazing. It is so immediately current, it could have been written today. In times of apostasy or coldness in the church, when it feels that the world has dismissed

Christianity and the church is not respected, academics have always turned to apologetics in an attempt to get the attention of skeptics. The very opposite is what is needed, but the flesh of Eve and the pride of Cain remain with us. With good reason Paul warned Timothy:

> **1 Timothy 6:20** O Timothy, keep that which is committed to thy trust, avoiding profane and vain babblings, and **oppositions of science falsely so called**:
> **21** Which some professing have erred concerning the faith. Grace be with thee. Amen.

Apparently in Paul's day some scientists formed arguments to oppose the faith, and were successful in causing some to err. How did Paul say they should respond to the science? **Avoid their "vain babblings."**

Evolutionists Hate Gap Creationism

Evolutionists, wanting to find a scientific reason to dismiss the Bible, are quite willing to agree with Creation Scientists that the Bible teaches a young earth and universe, and that Christians have always believed in a young earth. When your opponent in a debate assumes a position that is self-sabotaging, you tend to grin and be fully supportive. Evolutionists are grinning. With Scientific Creationists adamantly arguing for a young earth, evolutionists do not need to enter into any serious discussions on genetics and other weaknesses of evolution, for they can publicly dismiss Creationists and the Bible with ease by ridiculing the concept of a young earth and universe.

But evolutionists hate Gap Creationism because our position cannot be dismissed outright. If the Bible does not provide any statements as to the age of the earth, and Christians, knowing that the age of the earth has absolutely nothing to do with the evolutionary debate, do not try to contravene their conclusions concerning age, then the Bible cannot be dismissed on grounds of being anti-science. If the Bible allows for a much older universe, then evolutionists would have to stop ridiculing and start debating the issue of creation on the facts of science. So they are quite willing to take the position of Young Earthers in regarding Gap Creationism as a come-lately idea designed to answer evolution. It makes their campaign for public acceptance much easier by laughing Creationists of every stripe off the stage before the debate even begins. With no credible challenge to their position, and a belief that Christians have reinvented their creation views to fit the geological ages, they are comfortable as they continue to fornicate without feeling a threat from the Old Black Book. Young Earthers have fallen into a pit they have dug, and taken the rest of us with them.

So we Gap Creationists are flanked by evolutionists on one side and Young Earthers on the other, both deeming our argument most challenging to their positions. Of course they are not going to admit it, but **the amount of time these yokefellows put into challenging Gap Creationism is a sure indicator of how threatened they are by this biblical and historical doctrine.**

So we Bible-believing Gap Creationists, though flanked on both sides, are not outflanked, and we remain standing on the words of God as interpreted by ancient Hebrews and early Christians down to the present.

Young, Old, We're Not Told
So know that we Gap adherents do not reject the notion of a young earth, but neither do we insist upon it. Who is so

informed as to unravel the mystery of age when God has done everything in his power to make it **look** ancient? **Arguing for a young universe is arguing against the efforts of God to make it appear old.**

Now one may use empirical data to argue that the present ecosystem and geological stratification is of relatively young origin, and one may argue that it is much older. After all, academics who do not fish or hunt or tend to a garden and who don't have twenty-five grandkids probably do need something to occupy their time. But the rest of us ordinary Christians just don't care. If you think we do, you are confusing us with the small circle of academics engaging in speculative geology. **The definition of futility is a forensic geologist trying to draw a conclusion based on evidence God has tampered with.** He is very good at covering up the date of his creation.

The work of Creation Scientists in revealing the hand of the Creator in all things is a very valuable contribution to apologetics. And we have all been blessed by the truths of nature they have revealed, but they are not serving us well when they cause the world to think that Christians deny the apparent age of the solar system. Why argue against all appearances when **the important issue is the fact that it was all created instantly by the spoken word of an omnipotent God who has provided redemption in Jesus Christ?**

Reboot

Again, I feel sorry for the Anti-Gap crowd. I think they ran away with their theories before they coordinated with the Bible and history. They are now so heavily invested in their suppositions that it would require a complete abandonment of their vocation and their means of making a living if they were to accept biblical truth on the subject. Think how embarrassing it will be to say:

> "I am a scientist who is supposed to be objective, but I allowed my prejudices to run away with me, and for years I have advocated a theory based on my understanding of science. I still think I was right about the science of a young earth, but I know I was wrong to place my faith in my interpretation of science contrary to the Bible's clear articulation of a gap between the original creation and the six days of creation that followed the void state. I ask all those who have always believed the Bible just as it is written, whom I denigrated by suggesting they did disservice to the atonement, to forgive me. I have taken my twelve books off the market and will be pursuing a career as a carpenter. Thank you for your forgiveness."

We forgive you, but please don't retreat into the wonderful world of carpentry. It would be a great waste. You can still be of service to the church if you would utilize your scientific knowledge to expose the fallacies of evolution and present your arguments for a young earth. It would also be helpful if you would continue to give evidence for the impact of Noah's flood upon the geology of our planet. Just don't claim that the Bible teaches a young earth, and make sure everyone understands that your young earth views are just a theory. And while you are at it, you might investigate further that obscure little Bible verse that possibly indicates that after the flood, several generations before Abraham, the earth experienced a cataclysmic division (1 Chronicles 1:19). Go where your science leads you, but if it leads you to a position that would be contrary to Scripture, you will need to doubt your science until you can investigate further. I am confident that if you maintain prayerful objectivity, you will discover the perfect accuracy of Scripture and its complete harmony with verified science.

PERSONAL CONCLUSION

I must confess, when an old couple that does street preaching and ministers on college campuses challenged me to write this book, I was not up to date on the creation/evolution battle. My life has been filled with ministry and twenty-four grandkids. I began my research by reading everything I could find published by the Young Earthers, expecting the material to be quite challenging, and answering it to be difficult. But I was shocked to discover the absolute weakness of their arguments. I was even more shocked to discover the inaccuracies. I expected a lot more wisdom and discernment from the Christian Science movement. I had assumed that scientists would be objective. While I grew to be offended by their assault on Bible believers, I came to be embarrassed for them.

I have met some of the men I quoted in this book, and even shared a podium with one of them for several days. I found him to be quite a nice fellow and very congenial. He is a true Christian gentleman. But truth cannot consider the likability of the purveyor of an idea, nor even his integrity or intentions. Ideas, science, and Bible doctrine are bigger than the men who promote them. Some ideas and some doctrines are right and some are wrong. I have called the shots as they are without respect to the men who espouse them.

The men I have quoted as in error are not evil; they are just wrong. If my assertions prove to be wrong, they should be exposed with sound argument based on biblical interpretation. I may have made some errors and stand to be corrected. I will not take it personally when I receive your note pointing out my error. Again, ideas are bigger than any one man and deserve the careful scrutiny of any interested party.

But if you want to communicate with me on this issue, you had better hurry; I will be in the third heaven before long, waiting for the new heavens and the new earth wherein dwelleth righteousness.

USB Verse-by-Verse Bible Teaching Audio Library

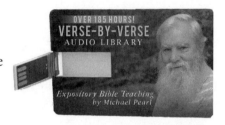

Over 185 hours of verse-by-verse Bible teaching. Plug and play in any USB port!

Romans Commentary

This popular commentary is a careful word-for-word examination fo the most important book in the Bible, addressing the hard, theological isues that have been the foundation of the Christian faith down through the centuries.

Free Download

Download Michael Pearl's complete and unabridged book of Romans audio series here: nogreaterjoy.org/audio/romans-audio/

Who is the Antichrist?

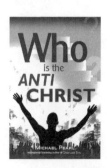

The biblical facts concerning antichrist are far different from popular belief. This little book will point you in the right direction and launch your study of this critical subject

ion 20
I saw the dead, small and
tand before God; and the
vere opened: and another
as opened, which is the
life: and the dead were
out of those things which
ritten in the books,
ng to their works.

THE DOOR

VERSE-BY-VERSE TEACHING ON YOUTUBE AND FACEBOOK

LIVESTREAM IN-DEPTH
BIBLE STUDIES

THURSDAYS AT 7:00 PM

PAST EPISODES AT:

acebook.com/TheDoorOfLobelville
outube.com/c/TheDoorMichaelPearl

LOBELVILLE, TN 37097

VIEW PAST
EPISODES AT
THESE LINKS!

Facebook.com/
TheDoorofLobelville

Youtube.com/c/
TheDoorMichaelPearl

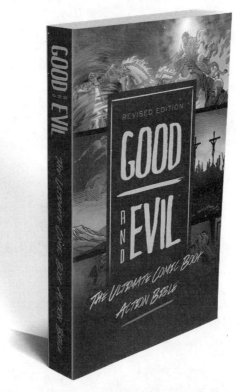